SUCCESS
by **Design**

Third Edition

Gabby McCutchen and Erin Riney

HAYDEN
HM
McNEIL

Hayden-McNeil Sustainability

Hayden-McNeil's standard paper stock uses a minimum of 30% post-consumer waste. We offer higher % options by request, including a 100% recycled stock. Additionally, Hayden-McNeil Custom Digital provides authors with the opportunity to convert print products to a digital format. Hayden-McNeil is part of a larger sustainability initiative through Macmillan Higher Ed. Visit http://sustainability.macmillan.com to learn more.

Printed in the United States of America

10 9 8 7 6 5 4 3 2 1

ISBN 978-0-7380-7001-8

Hayden-McNeil Publishing
14903 Pilot Drive
Plymouth, MI 48170
www.hmpublishing.com

McCutchen 7001-8 F14

Table of Contents

Introduction:
Getting a Good Start

Congratulations on enrolling in ACA! This class will help you prepare for academic success at your college and beyond. *Success by Design* has been written to accompany what you learn from the class through the inclusion of content and practice activities customized for North Carolina community college students.

Success by Design and your ACA course will provide a useful structure to learn more about yourself, your college, and learning strategies. While you likely already have some knowledge of these topics, it is often difficult to prioritize the reflection and research necessary to further develop your awareness and skills on your own. *Success by Design* and your ACA class will provide you with expert instruction in academic and career goal discernment, learning strategies, and college culture to take your knowledge to the next level.

Many NC community colleges require ACA for degrees or diplomas because college success classes like ACA have proven to be very important to student persistence and success, as national research tells us. In fact, data from within our state indicates that students taking and passing ACA with at least a C are more likely to return to the college the next semester. And that's exactly what your college's faculty, staff, and administrators want to see—students coming back semester after semester to earn the credits necessary for a college credential. Succeeding in this class will lay a foundation for success in future courses.

As you prepare for academic success this semester, have a look at the Table of Contents and note the concepts you will be discussing through this class. Flip through the book to see how you might augment your knowledge and become prepared to meet college expectations. Notice, too, the large margins, which provide plenty of room for you to take notes easily, and the end of chapter questions, which will review important chapter concepts. You'll also find helpful tracking sheets to personalize your learning and strategies as well as trouble-shooting tables, sidebars, and bolded terms with critical information and tips. Throughout *Success by Design*, you'll find useful information and strategies that you can start to apply immediately to guarantee your college success.

Begin planning for your success today!

UNIT 1
Goal Discernment

Goal discernment is the deliberate and systematic process of examining yourself and your options to make informed decisions about your future. You can apply the stages of goal discernment to make decisions about your academic and career goals. In fact, you may have already moved through the stages of goal discernment without realizing the benefits of the full process. If you are attending college after several years in the workforce, then you likely have already given some thought to what you like and dislike doing professionally. And if you are a recent high school graduate, then you may have done some research and academic writing on your potential careers. This unit of *Success by Design* will potentially strengthen or challenge your goals. The four chapters in this unit will prepare you for each of the three stages of goal discernment.

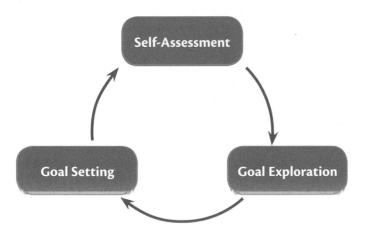

Chapter 1 Self-Assessment

First of all, you must assess yourself. What are your interests? What are your values? What are you good at? What is your ideal balance of your work and your personal life? How long are you willing to be a student? At this stage, you focus on your personality, your interests, and your values.

Chapter 2 Academic Goal Exploration

Second of all, you must do some research. What credentials are available to you at your community college? What are your options for transfer to a senior institution? What certification or training is required for your career interests? This stage of the process requires that you do some research about your academic choices.

Chapter 3 Career Goal Exploration

In addition to researching your academic options, you need to explore your career options. What is the job outlook? What is the starting salary? What opportunities for advancement exist? This chapter will complement the resources you discover in Chapter 2 but will focus on your professional choices.

Chapter 4 Goal Setting

Finally, you take action by setting goals based on your self-assessments and research. This chapter emphasizes the benefits of SMART goals. You'll also find resources to help you achieve your academic goals in a timely and thoughtful manner.

Important Learning Outcomes for Unit 1

- Identify your learning style preferences and strategies to support your learning style preferences.

- Research careers that match your personality traits, interests, and work values.

- Develop a strategic plan for completing community college academic goals, including certificates, diplomas, and/or associate degrees.

- Identify the rights and responsibilities of transfer students under the Comprehensive Articulation Agreement (CAA), including Universal General Education Transfer Component (UGETC) designated courses, the Transfer Assured Admissions Policy (TAAP), the CAA appeals process, and university tuition surcharge.

- Write academic goals that are specific, measurable, attainable, realistic, and time-bound.

Unit 1: Goal Discernment Tracking Sheet

As you read Unit 1, record the individual elements of your personal goal discernment in the table below. This will be a helpful record to track your personalized preferences and plans.

Holland Code/ Interest Profiler Results	Top 3–5 Work Values
Program of Study or Major and Related Career Options	**Learning Style Preferences**
SMART Academic Goals	**SMART Professional Goals**

STUDENT NOTES

Self-Assessment

As you learned in the introduction to Unit 1, self-assessment is often the first stage in the cycle of goal discernment. **Self-assessment** is the systematic reflection on who you are as a person. Specifically, what are your interests, personality traits, and values? And how can these traits best inform your goals?

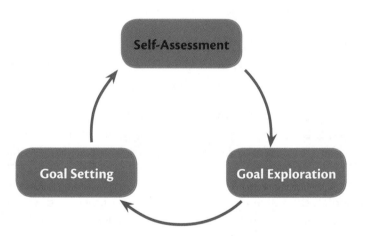

When you match your interests, personality, and values to your academic and professional goals, you can expect to be fulfilled both professionally and personally by your choices. You will feel satisfied with your choices and motivated to go to work even on days when you are tired or experiencing a disagreement with a co-worker. When you choose a career based on thorough self-assessment, these small distractions remain small distractions and your professional motivation remains high.

Many of us make decisions about our academic programs and future careers based on our superficial understanding of our own interests, personality, and values. But few of us take the time to be deliberate about identifying what exactly makes us unique and then search for academic programs and careers that suit us. The activities that follow will help you deliberately assess yourself, so you can make informed decisions (or confirm the decisions you have already made) about your goals.

Specifically, Chapter 1 includes the following useful self-assessment topics:

- personality and interests,
- work values, and
- learning styles.

Personality and Interests

The most common first step in self-assessment is to examine your personality and interests. Many college students choose their academic programs and future career paths based on their interests. For example, individuals who enjoy writing and following current events naturally become interested in journalism or media communications. Similarly, individuals who like a structured workday with few surprises may naturally become interested in careers like accounting or medical assisting. You can apply the information about Holland Codes on the next few pages and on the College Foundation of North Carolina (CFNC) website to explore your personality and interests as they relate to academic or career choices.

Holland Codes are a widely known and well-respected personality and interest assessment. Dr. John Holland, a psychologist, identified the six personality types in the Holland Codes that can be combined into 720 different patterns.

The hexagon on the following page shows the relationships of the personality types to one another. The codes closest together are more alike; the codes opposite from each other are least alike. For example, artistic individuals are not likely to also have many conventional characteristics (opposite) but will likely find they have several investigative and social preferences (closest). Most people are a combination of types, and the combinations usually correspond with each other on the hexagon.

These types refer to both individual personalities and workplace environments. For example, a person's Holland Code might be CRI (**C**onventional, **R**ealistic, and **I**nvestigative) or SEA (**S**ocial, **E**nterprising, and **A**rtistic). Likewise, a specific career might be categorized as Conventional or Artistic.

Career counselors recommend identifying your personal Holland Code and then using your Holland Code to find similar work environments. People who work in environments that match their personality types are more likely to feel satisfied in their work lives. For example, if you have a very social personality, then not surprisingly you would prefer a workplace in which you have a lot of interaction with co-workers and/or the public. You might feel dissatisfied in a workplace where you must work independently with little opportunities to interact with other people.

Once you determine your Holland Code, use the table below to identify your compatible work environments. Notice that the compatibility is determined by the location on the hexagon. See the "Step 2: Match Your Holland Code to Compatible Careers" on page 9 for specific examples of careers.

Personality Type	Most Compatible Careers	Other Compatible Careers
Realistic	Realistic	Investigative and Conventional
Investigative	Investigative	Realistic and Artistic
Artistic	Artistic	Investigative and Social
Social	Social	Artistic and Enterprising
Enterprising	Enterprising	Social and Conventional
Conventional	Conventional	Enterprising and Realistic

STUDENT NOTES

You can also figure out your Holland Code by completing the Interest Profiler activity on the CFNC website.

See the instructions on how to log in to CFNC and access the Interest Profiler on page 14.

Step 1: Identify Your Holland Code

Read the descriptions below and decide which personality type defines you the best. Next, choose which would be the second and third best descriptions of your personality. Write the three letters below. This is your Holland Code:

——— ——— ———

R – Realistic People (Doers)

They like to work with machines, and they often like to work with their hands to build things. Their skills include having mechanical know-how, stamina to work outdoors, and the ability to operate machinery. They are often practical, love nature, and are good problem-solvers. They like working with things and tools.

I – Investigative People (Thinkers)

They like to explore ideas and analyze data. They have skills in math and science. Inquisitive, precise, and sometimes abstract thinking are characteristics of their personality. They like working with data and ideas.

A – Artistic People (Creators)

They like to create, sing, dance, or write and prefer an unstructured work environment. They have skills in music, art, and/or communication. They value aesthetic qualities and are more likely to relate by indirect means through their medium. They like working with ideas.

C – Conventional People (Organizers)

They like an organized and detail-oriented workplace. They are often skilled in finance, mathematics, and keyboarding. They see themselves as conforming, organized, and practical. They like working with data.

E – Enterprising People (Persuaders)

They like to persuade and influence others in areas of business or politics. They perceive themselves as popular, self-confident, and social. They have skills in public speaking and leadership. Enterprising types like working with people and data.

S – Social People (Helpers)

They enjoy helping others and the community. They have skills in teaching, counseling, and getting along with others, and are sensitive to others' needs. They are cheerful, scholarly, and verbally oriented. They like working with people.

Step 2: Match Your Holland Code to Compatible Careers

Every profession requires more than just one talent. The chart below organizes each career or workplace environment by its main characteristic only. Remember that according to the theory behind the Holland Codes, you should look for a workplace environment that is compatible with your personal Holland Code.

R – Realistic People (Doers)

engineer, broadcast technician, landscape worker, barber, fire fighter, cook, auto mechanic, carpenter, surgical technologist, machinist, heavy truck driver, pest control worker, air traffic controller, roofer

I – Investigative People (Thinkers)

computer programmer, conservation scientist, financial analyst, microbiologist, physician, physician's assistant, pharmacist, chemist, biomedical engineer, food scientist, veterinarian, natural sciences manager, geologist, anthropologist, lab technician

C – Conventional People (Organizers)

bookkeeper, accountant, tax preparer, court reporter, cashiers, paralegal, bank teller, insurance underwriter, medical records technician, secretary/office worker, building inspector, computer operator

A – Artistic People (Creators)

commercial artist, singer, actor/actress, editor, author, music teacher, journalist, graphic designer, advertising manager, floral designer, animator, museum curator, photographer

E – Enterprising People (Persuaders)

salesperson, financial manager, construction manager, sports promoter, convention manager, lawyer, politician, real estate agent, marketing manager, business executive

S – Social People (Helpers)

nurse, physical therapist, occupational therapy assistant, teacher or teacher assistant, aerobics instructor, social worker, clergy, coach, dental hygienist, counselor, probation officer, paramedic, personnel director, home health aide

R I
C A
E S

This list is obviously incomplete. Not every career is listed here. However, based on the careers that are listed, you can start to identify the characteristics of the individual careers that explain their categorization into a specific Holland Code category.

You can also log on to CFNC.org for additional career suggestions based on your Holland Code.

When you explore career options on well-recognized websites such as CFNC and O*NET, you'll find careers organized by these Holland Code categories even if the websites don't refer to Holland Codes specifically. Knowing your Holland Code will help you efficiently search for compatible academic programs and careers.

STUDENT NOTES

You can also identify your work values by completing the Work Values Sorter activity on the CFNC website.

See the instructions on how to log on to CFNC and access the Work Values Sorter on page 14.

Work Values

While it may be obvious to choose an academic program or career field based on your personality and interests, less obvious—but equally important—is the connection between your academic program or career field and your work values. Your **work values** are the elements of your personal belief system that are fulfilled from your career or workplace. If, for example, you value variety or challenging work experiences, then you may become bored in a career that requires repetitive, simplistic work. Identifying your work values (like knowing your Holland Code) will help you make deliberate decisions about your future career. Not surprisingly, if you choose a career that matches your work values, then you are more likely to feel satisfied by your work.

Complete the following self-assessment to identify what types of satisfaction you expect from your work.

Step 1: Identify Your Work Values

Read the following list of satisfying results that individuals report getting from their careers. Rate the importance of each category using the following scale:

> 1 Unimportant or undesirable
> 2 Somewhat important
> 3 Very important to you in your career/job

___ **Advancement:** Have opportunities to work hard and move ahead in my organization

___ **Affiliation:** Be recognized as being associated with a particular organization

___ **Artistic:** Be involved in creative works of art, music, literature, drama, decorating, or other art forms

___ **Authority:** Have control over others' work activities and be able to partially affect their destinies

___ **Be Needed:** Feel that what I do is necessary for the survival or welfare of others

___ **Beauty:** Have a job which involves the aesthetic appreciation of the study of things, ideas, or people

___ **Community:** Work at a job in which I can get involved in community affairs

___ **Competition:** Pit my abilities against those of others in situations which test my competencies and in which there are win or lose outcomes

___ **Contact with People:** Have regular contact with the public

___ **Creative Expression:** Have opportunities to express my ideas, reactions, and observations about my work and how I might improve it verbally or in writing

___ **Creativity:** Create new programs and systems; develop original structures and procedures not dependent on someone else's format

___ **Decision-Making:** Have the power to decide policies, agendas, courses of action, etc.

___ **Exercise Competence:** Have opportunities to involve myself in those areas in which I feel I have talents above the average person

___ **Expertise:** Be respected and sought after for my knowledge and skills in a given area

___ **Fun:** Work in a situation in which I am free to be spontaneous, playful, humorous, and exuberant

___ **Help Society:** Make a contribution for the betterment of the world in which I live

___ **Helping Others:** Provide a service to and assist others as individuals or as groups

___ **High-Income Possibilities:** Work, which can lead to substantial earnings or profit, enables me to purchase essential items and the luxuries of life I desire

___ **Independence:** Be able to direct and control the course of my work, determining its nature without a great deal of direction from others

___ **Influence:** Be able to change and influence others' attitudes or opinions

___ **Integration:** Be able to integrate my working life with my personal life, involving my family or close friends

___ **Job Tranquility:** Avoid pressure and the "rat race"

___ **Intellectual Status:** Be recognized as a person with high intellectual ability; one who is an authority in a given area of knowledge

___ **Learning:** Be able to continually learn new skills and acquire new knowledge and understanding

11

____ **Location:** Live in a place which is conducive to my lifestyle and in which I can do the activities I enjoy

____ **Moral/Spiritual:** Have a sense that my work is important to and in accord with a set of standards in which I believe

____ **Orderliness of Environment:** Work in a consistently ordered environment where everything has its place and things are not changed often

____ **Personal Growth and Development:** Engage in work which offers me opportunity to grow as a person

____ **Physical Work Environment:** Work in a place which is pleasing to me aesthetically or beautiful to me

____ **Physical:** Do work which makes physical demands and in which I can use my coordination and physical abilities

____ **Predictability:** Have a stable and relatively unchanging work routine and job duties

____ **Pressure:** Have a job which involves working against time deadlines and/or where others critique the quality of my work

____ **Problem Solving:** Have a position that provides challenging problems to solve and avoids routine

____ **Productive:** Produce tangibles, things I can see and touch

____ **Recognition:** Be visibly and publicly appreciated and given credit for the quality of my work

____ **Relationships:** Develop close friendships with my co-workers and other people I meet in the course of my work activities

____ **Responsibility:** Be responsible for the planning and implementation of many tasks and projects as well as for the people involved

____ **Risk Taking:** Have work which requires me to take risks or accept challenges frequently

____ **Security:** Be able to depend on keeping my job and making enough money

____ **Status:** Have a position which carries respect with my friends, family, and community

____ **Supervision:** Be directly responsible for work which is done and produced by others under my supervision

___ **Time Freedom:** Be free to plan and manage my own time schedule in work; be able to set my own hours

___ **Undemanding:** Have work duties which demand very little energy or involvement

___ **Uniqueness:** Feel that the work I do is unique, novel, and different from others in some way

___ **Variety:** Do a number of different tasks; have the setting and content of my work responsibilities change frequently

___ **Work Alone:** Work by myself on projects and tasks

___ **Work on Frontiers of Knowledge:** Be involved in hard science of human research; work in a company that is considered one of the best in the business and strive for advances

___ **Work with Others:** Be a member of a working team; work with others in a group toward common goals

Step 2: Prioritize Your Work Values

Look back at the numbers you assigned to the individual work values on the previous pages. Note the values to which you assigned a "3." Now list below the three values that you would not be willing to compromise beginning with your most valued. These are your personal work values that should guide your academic and career goal exploration as well as your goal setting.

1. _____

2. _____

3. _____

This work values self-assessment was adapted from an activity used by SOICC—North Carolina's Career Resource Network. For more information about SOICC, see www.soicc.state.nc.us.

As you explore potential majors and potential careers, keep your work values in mind and look for opportunities to match your values to your goals. In the same way that individuals who work in fields that are compatible with their personalities and interests can expect job satisfaction, people who seek out careers that fit their work values can expect to be personally and professional satisfied by their careers.

College Foundation of North Carolina

The College Foundation of North Carolina (CFNC) website features several useful self-assessment tools. Specifically, CFNC allows students to complete interactive, self-scoring exercises that identify their personality and interests and their work values. Then the website identifies possible careers that match the self-assessment results. Additionally, CFNC is a useful tool for goal exploration as you'll learn in Chapters 2 and 3.

Create a free CFNC.org account by following the directions below.

Step 1: Open an Internet Browser and Go to the College Foundation of North Carolina Website: www.cfnc.org

Notice all of the available links on the CFNC homepage. You can apply to North Carolina universities and colleges, research scholarships, investigate North Carolina careers, and track your progress through your college classes.

Step 2: Log on to My CFNC

If you used the CFNC website to apply for financial aid or apply for admission to your college, then enter your username and password.

If you are new to the CFNC website, then click on the "CREATE MY CFNC ACCOUNT" link to create a username and password for this website.

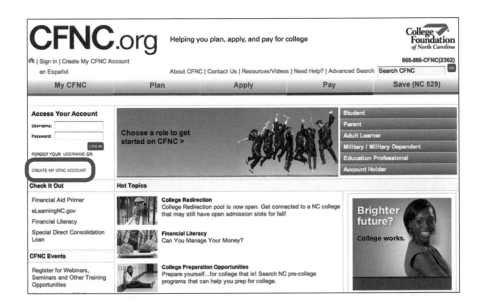

Step 3: Select "College or Postsecondary School Student"

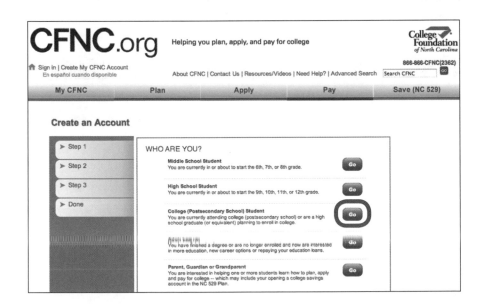

STUDENT NOTES

Step 4: Enter Your College as Your Post-Secondary School

Click on the "Find" button to open the School Finder window. Find your college in the alphabetical list and click on it. Then click on "Submit."

When the name of your college appears in the search field, click on "Next."

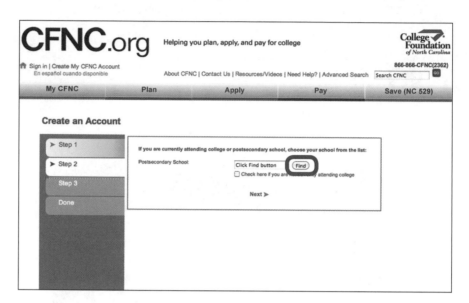

You will have to create a username and password on this page.

For your username, choose something that will be easy for you to remember, such as the first part of another college account like your school email address. Choose something you will easily remember for your password, too.

At the bottom of the page, you can type a question and answer that the website can use to send you your password if you ever forget it. Again, choose something easy to remember.

Step 5: Complete the "Create an Account" Page

Type in your personal information and create a CFNC account and password. Notice that you must type in a permanent address and mailing address even if they are the same.

Step 6: Select "Click here to continue"

When you are finished, you'll receive a message stating "You have successfully created your account." Click on the link "Click here to continue."

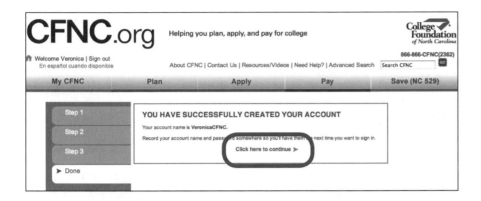

Step 7: Click on "Plan" > "For A Career"

When you put your cursor over "Plan," an orange line with new links appears. Click on "For A Career."

Step 8: Click "Learn About Yourself"

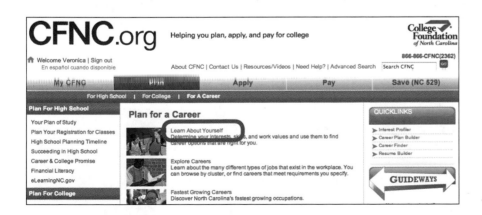

Step 9: Orient Yourself to the "Learn About Yourself" Page

Notice the two assessments at the top of the page. Complete the Interest Profiler and Work Values Sorter. The Interest Profiler will tell you your Holland Code (see the descriptions of the Holland Codes earlier in this chapter for more information). The Work Values Sorter will tell you your top two or three work values. Specifically, the Work Values Sorter will indicate your preferences for the following work values: Recognition, Relationships, Achievement, Support, Independence, and Working Conditions.

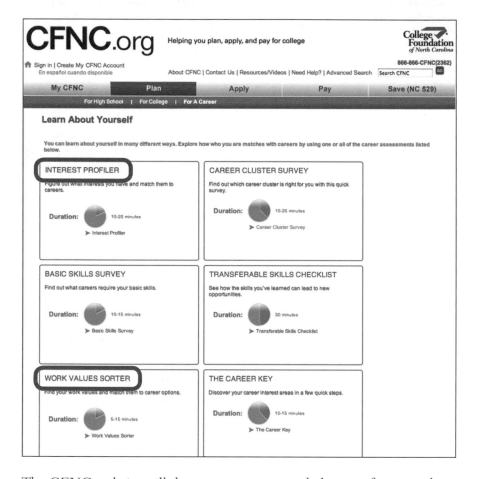

The CFNC website will then report careers and clusters of careers that match your interests and your values. You can click on "View Careers" to find these matches.

You can then find information on the skills and requirements necessary for the jobs listed as well as average pay (for North Carolina and the United States), job outlook, related careers, and important links. You can refine the search based on your preferences in these areas (for example, only careers that have an expected increase in demand).

Step 10: Click on "Sign Out"

When you finish working in CFNC, click on "Sign Out" before you close the Internet browser. By signing out and logging in the next time you use the site, the site will save your information.

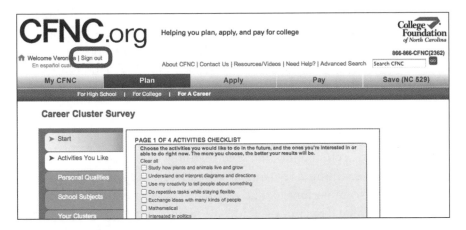

Sometimes students find that their results on the CFNC inventories do not match the decisions that they have previously made about their academic and career goals. For example, a student might feel strongly that he wants to be a nurse, but not find the career of nursing matches his interests and work values. If this is your experience, then you might use the CFNC website to explore careers that you hadn't previously considered that better match your self-assessment results. Or you might consider interpreting your self-assessment results a little more broadly.

This information provided on the CFNC website will help you transition to the next steps in goal discernment: academic and career goal exploration.

Learning Styles

Your **learning style** is your preferred method for learning new information. Identifying your learning style is a critical step in metacognition (thinking about how you learn). Your college instructors expect you to take responsibility for your own learning and to be able to learn in a laboratory or clinical setting, in study groups, in online learning environments, and in individual study as well as in the classroom. Everyone has natural learning style preferences, and knowing your learning style provides you with the opportunity to take advantage of your natural strengths as a learner. Understanding your learning style preferences will help you improve your study habits and make sense of difficult subjects.

As you read about the learning style typologies below and complete a learning styles inventory, keep in mind that your learning style indicates your preference along a continuum. No one has exclusively only one learning style preference. It is important to take advantage of your natural preferences to make learning easy; however, it is also important to be able to adapt to learning environments that don't match your natural preferences. Savvy college students not only know their learning style preference, but they also try out less-preferred learning styles to accommodate certain types of class formats or instructors' teaching styles.

Sensory Preferences

Learning styles are commonly organized into **sensory preferences**: visual, verbal, kinesthetic, and multi-modal. As you read the descriptions of each of the sensory preferences below, think about your personal sensory preferences.

Visual learners prefer visual representations of information (for example, charts, diagrams, pictures) to help them understand new ideas. They like instructors who show visual aids on the board or in PowerPoint slides. They also like textbooks that are printed in color and that have lots of pictures. Visual learners frequently highlight their textbooks and notes, and they use symbols in their notes to signify important concepts. When they take tests, visual learners can often remember information in a chart or graph more easily than information in sentences and paragraphs.

Verbal learners prefer lecture and discussion format classes. They may not take very good notes because they are so busy listening to the instructor and their classmates. When they study, they may read or quiz themselves out loud. Verbal learners frequently like to use tape recorders or digital recorders in class, so they can listen to the recording later to study the class content. They also like to participate in discussions either in class or with their instructors or classmates outside of class. When they see a chart or diagram, they have to translate the meaning into words, and then they often remember the explanations better than the chart or diagram.

Kinesthetic learners prefer to learn through using all of their senses (sight, touch, taste, smell, and hearing) and through hands-on, real-world applications. Kinesthetic learners often do not fully understand a concept until they can try it out for themselves in a laboratory or clinical setting. They like for their instructors to give them lots of examples of new ideas, and they often remember the examples and their experiences better than they remember a list of vocabulary terms or other forms of concrete knowledge.

Multi-modal learners have some combination of visual, verbal, and kinesthetic learning style preferences. Multi-modal learners may have any two of the sensory preferences (for example, visual and kinesthetic or verbal and kinesthetic). Or they may have all three sensory preferences (visual, verbal, and kinesthetic). These combinations of learning style preferences give multi-modal learners great flexibility in learning in several different types of learning environments. While the student with the very strong visual preference may struggle in a lecture-only class, the multi-modal visual-verbal learner can more easily adapt to the lecture format.

Hemispheric Dominance

Another common learning style typology describes individuals' brain **hemispheric dominance**, or right-brain and left-brain preferences. The human brain is divided into two hemispheres with very different functions that work together for all types of thinking, learning, and activity. The two sides are described in very general terms below. As you read the descriptions of right-brained people and left-brained people, think about which side of the brain best describes how you think and, therefore, hints at your personal hemispheric dominance.

The left side of the brain is responsible for use of language as well as logical and sequential thinking. **Left-brained** people typically pay attention to the steps in a process (for example, solving a math problem) or the details in a task (for example, spelling and grammar in writing an essay). Left-brained people also like using a checklist and completing tasks in a logical and sequential order. They have to understand the individual details of a new concept in order to understand the big picture.

The right side of the brain, on the other hand, processes visual input and is attentive to colors. **Right-brained** people are typically intuitive and global thinkers who rely on their instincts over methodical problem solving. Right-brained people resist making lists or schedules. They also prefer to work at their own pace and on what interests them in the moment, which can make them appear to be easily distracted. They can see a new concept's big picture readily and need to fully understand the big picture in order to be able to make meaning of its details.

Again, no one is exclusively left-brained or right-brained. But many of us do have a dominant hemisphere. You may find that you approach your college classes in a very left-brained logical, sequential way because college is so important to your personal goals and values. But in your personal life, you may prefer right-brained thinking.

Index of Learning Styles Questionnaire

You can probably identify your sensory and hemispheric preferences and patterns based on the simplistic definitions on the previous pages. However, you may have additional learning style preferences that you are unaware of. To more thoroughly identify the ways in which you learn best, complete the **Index of Learning Styles (ILS)** questionnaire, a learning styles preferences questionnaire developed by two professors at North Carolina State University. Your results on the ILS will give you a comprehensive picture of your learning style, including some sensory preferences (for example, visual-verbal) and some hemispheric dominance preferences (for example, sequencing-global and sensing-intuitive). It also measures your preferences in active and reflective learning.

Access the Index of Learning Styles questionnaire at the following link: http://www.engr.ncsu.edu/learningstyles/ilsweb.html.

If after you complete the ILS, you are interested in knowing more about your personal learning style preferences, search online for the following well-known learning styles inventories and questionnaires:

- VARK Learning Styles Inventory,
- Howard Gardner's Multiple Intelligences, and
- Myers-Briggs Type Indicator.

When you complete the 44-question ILS, print your Learning Styles Results Form and examine your results carefully. You'll see your results reported along the same scales in the example on the next page. Notice that your learning styles are reported along four continuums. Look for an X printed along each continuum. You may find that you have some strong preferences (for example, the score of 9 on the ACT end of the first continuum indicates a strong preference for active learning). Or you may learn that you are well balanced on one or more continuums (for example, the score of 1 on the VRB side of the third continuum on the next page).

NC STATE UNIVERSITY

Learning Styles Results

Results for: Sample Student

```
ACT         X                                                   REF
     11   9   7   5   3   1   1   3   5   7   9   11
                            <-- -->

SEN                 X                                           INT
     11   9   7   5   3   1   1   3   5   7   9   11
                            <-- -->

VIS                             X                               VRB
     11   9   7   5   3   1   1   3   5   7   9   11
                            <-- -->

SEQ                     X                                       GLO
     11   9   7   5   3   1   1   3   5   7   9   11
                            <-- -->
```

- If your score on a scale is 1–3, you are fairly well balanced on the two dimensions of that scale.

- If your score on a scale is 5–7, you have a moderate preference for one dimension of the scale and will learn more easily in a teaching environment which favors that dimension.

- If your score on a scale is 9–11, you have a very strong preference for one dimension of the scale. You may have real difficulty learning in an environment which does not support that preference.

We suggest you print this page, so that when you look at the explanations of the different scales you will have a record of your individual preferences.

For explanations of the scales and the implications of your preferences, click on **Learning Style Descriptions**.

For more information about learning styles or to take the test again, click on **Learning Style Page**.

After you note your learning styles preferences as reported by the Index of Learning Styles, read the descriptions of each of the scales on the next pages to better understand your learning style preferences. You can read more thorough descriptions of each of the scales on the ILS website.

Keep your learning style preferences and these study recommendations in mind when you read Chapter 8: Study Strategies.

	Active Learners	Reflective Learners
Characteristics	• Understand information when they discuss, apply, or explain it to someone else. • Prefer group work to solve a problem. • Prefer to manipulate objects, do physical experiments, and learn by trying.	• Understand information when they can think about it quietly first. • Prefer to work alone to solve a problem. • Prefer to think things through, to evaluate options, and learn by analysis.
Recommendations	• Study in a group. • Find ways to apply new information, such as creating a practice test and quizzing other classmates.	• Don't just read and memorize material; think about how you could apply new information. • Summarize or restate your class notes in your own words.

	Sensing Learners	Intuitive Learners
Characteristics	• Like to learn facts. • Like solving problems using regular methods; dislike surprises. • Prefer concrete, practical, and procedural information.	• Like to discover relationships and possibilities. • Like innovation; dislike repetition. • Prefer conceptual, innovative, and theoretical information that provides overall meaning.
Recommendations	• Look for specific examples of ideas or concepts. • Find ways to apply new information to your own life. • Ask your instructor for applications to the real world.	• Look for connections between ideas. • Take the time to read and think about a question before you start answering it. • Take your time on tests; don't get impatient with details or checking your work.

	Visual Learners	Verbal Learners
Characteristics	• Remember what they see—pictures, graphs, diagrams, films, demonstrations. • Prefer visual representations of information.	• Remember words—what they hear and what they read. • Prefer to hear or read information. • Look for explanations with words.
Recommendations	• Find charts or other visual representation of new material. • Color-code your notes so all related topics are one color. • Create concept maps to organize new ideas.	• Write summaries or outlines of notes in your own words. • Work in groups to talk about lessons.

Sequential Learners	Global Learners
Characteristics • Understand ideas in linear steps. • Follow steps to find solutions. • Prefer to have information presented linearly and in an orderly manner. • Put together the details in order to see the big picture.	• Learn in large jumps without knowing how ideas relate. • Suddenly "get" it. • Can solve problems in new ways, but can't always explain how they did it. • Prefer a holistic and systematic approach to learning. • See the big picture first and then fill in the details.
Recommendations • Outline lecture material in logical order. • Improve your global thinking skills by relating new ideas to things you already know. • Ask an instructor who skips from topic to topic to fill in any missed steps or missed material.	• Before you read a chapter, skim it to see the big picture. • Study the same subject for extended periods of time. • Be patient; it may be harder for you to understand the smaller pieces of a big concept.

Conclusion

After you have completed the multiple self-assessments described in this chapter, you should have a clearer understanding of who you are as a college student and a future professional. Whereas you may have had a vague idea of your personality, interests, and values previously, you can now describe these components of yourself using language that is common to career search and goal discernment. Similarly, you identified your learning style preferences by completing the Index of Learning Styles. These academic self-assessments can inform your goals, too, and can prepare you for long-term academic success.

Don't forget to record your Holland Code, work values, and learning style preferences on page 3 for easy reference.

STUDENT NOTES

CHAPTER 1
Self-Assessment

1. Look again at the descriptions in your Holland Code. What descriptions of your personality and interests are most accurate for you? What descriptions are not accurate? What one word best describes your codes?

2. In addition to your interests and values, what else should you take into consideration when choosing a career? List five questions that would contribute to the self-assessment stage of goal discernment.

3. Compare the results of your Holland Codes self-analysis on page 8 and the results of the Interest Profiler on the CFNC website. How are they similar? If they are different, then which one is more accurate?

4. How well does your intended career match your interests and personality (as determined by the Holland Codes and/or CFNC website)? Identify the specific aspects of your interests that your career will help you fulfill.

5. Compare the results of your Work Values self-analysis on page 13 and the results of the Work Values Sorter on the CFNC website. How are they similar? If they are different, then which one is more accurate?

6. How well does your intended career match your work values? Identify your work values that will be achieved in your chosen career.

7. Jasmine is a first-semester college student who is struggling in her developmental math class. She always did well in math classes in high school, but she hasn't been in a math classroom in over 10 years, and she can't remember much from high school algebra. She knows that her strongest learning style preferences are visual, sensing, and active. Which of the three learning style preferences will help her most in developmental math? Why? What is one strategy specific to that learning style that she should try?

8. Anthony is taking SPA 111 (Elementary Spanish I) and SPA 181 (Spanish Lab I) for the second time this semester. He dropped the classes last semester after he failed the first two tests. In one week, he will take his first test in Spanish this semester. He knows that his strongest learning style preferences are verbal and intuitive. Which of the two learning style preferences will help him most in preparing for the Spanish test? Why? What is one strategy specific to that learning style that he should try?

9. One common study technique that works for college students with different learning style preferences is flash cards. Fill in the table below with two strategies for visual learners to use flash cards and two strategies for verbal learners to use flash cards.

How visual learners can use flash cards effectively	How verbal learners can use flash cards effectively

10. Another common study technique that works for college students with different learning style preferences is writing practice test questions. Fill in the table below with two strategies for active learners to use practice tests and two strategies for reflective learners to use practice tests.

How active learners can use practice tests effectively	How reflective learners can use practice tests effectively

Academic Goal Exploration

N ow that you have clear definitions of your interests and values, it's time to explore your options. This means research. To ensure that you are on the right academic and career path, you need to research your goal options and look for connections to what you've learned about yourself in the self-assessment stage of goal discernment. This chapter of *Success by Design* will introduce you to several resources and concepts to help you move through the goal exploration stage of goal discernment. Specifically, it will focus on academic goal exploration.

As you consider your academic options, you should learn as much as you can about your chosen academic program and other related academic programs. Goals change, and the cycles of goal discernment are perennial. Therefore, you may change your program or pursue additional programs based on what you learn from your research.

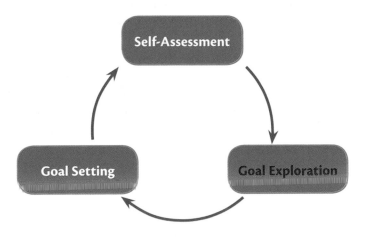

Chapter 2 will address the following very useful tools in academic goal exploration:

- Community college credentials;
- Programs of Study;
- Plans of Study, Major Pathways, Pre-Majors, Study Tracks;
- Three options for transfer to senior institutions; and
- College Foundation of North Carolina (CFNC).

Community College Credentials

Many colleges offer both AAS and AA/AS degrees in many of the same fields. For example, students who are interested in business careers may pursue an AAS degree or an AA degree. Business students who want to enter their new career fields immediately after graduation from the community college should pursue the AAS degree. Business students who want to transfer to a university and eventually earn a bachelor's degree should pursue the AA degree.

If your desired career has both an AA/AS degree option and an AAS degree option, then consider how the different degrees will factor into your career focus and responsibilities.

Community colleges are unique institutions of higher education because they follow an **open door with guided placement policy** that allows them to admit any student who has earned a high school credential or its equivalent. Because community colleges do not have competitive admissions, most community colleges require some placement testing to make sure that students are prepared for the college-level coursework in their programs. **Placement tests** commonly assess students' writing, reading, and math skills; students' scores indicate what classes they can begin taking. Later in this chapter, you will learn more about pre-requisite courses called developmental education courses that many students must take based on their placement test results.

Students attend community colleges for a variety of reasons. Some students want to complete a degree or other short credential to prepare for a new career, such as Clinical Trials Research Associate or Networking Technologies. Other students choose to attend community colleges to earn a transferable associate degree before they move on to a senior four-year college or university, like North Carolina Central University or University of North Carolina–Greensboro. Still others take classes off and on for personal enrichment or because they haven't yet decided on a career or educational path.

Community colleges offer a variety of credentials that meet all of these goals. Most community college students are working toward an associate degree. North Carolina's community colleges offer Associate in Applied Science (AAS), Associate in Arts (AA), Associate in Science (AS), Associate in Fine Arts (AFA), and Associate in General Education (AGE). Check with your college to see which of these degrees are available to you.

Career and technical education students and health technologies students frequently enroll in **Associate in Applied Science (AAS)** programs. The Associate in Applied Science degree includes some general education courses, but it primarily focuses on major courses that prepare students for a new career. Common Associate in Applied Science programs include Nursing, Automotive Technology, Occupational Therapy Assistant, and Early Childhood Education.

University transfer students work toward the **Associate in Arts (AA)**, **Associate in Science (AS)**, or **Associate in Fine Arts (AFA)** degree, depending on what they plan to major in at the senior institution. For example, students who plan to major in social work, education, psychology, or business are Associate in Arts students. Students who plan to major in biology, chemistry, math, or engineering are Associate in Science students. Students who plan to major in music and music education, art, or drama are Associate in Fine Arts students. Of the 58 North Carolina community colleges, all offer AA degrees, 57 offer AS degrees, and 36 offer AFA degrees as of Spring 2014.

Finally, students who want to take classes for their own personal growth earn the **Associate in General Education (AGE)** degree. The Associate in General Education degree does not prepare students for a new career, nor does it transfer to a senior institution. Of the 58 North Carolina community colleges, 53 offer AGE degrees.

In addition to degrees, community colleges offer **diploma** programs which require 36–48 credit hours. Diplomas often prepare students for specific careers, such as Licensed Practical Nursing and Surgical Technology. All 58 North Carolina community colleges offer diplomas.

Community colleges also offer **certificates** that are shorter credentials that typically demonstrate necessary requirements for professional certifications. Often students earn certificates as they work toward a diploma or associate degree. For example, a student may earn an Engine Performance Certificate as he completes the Automotive Technology program. Certificates require 12–18 credit hours. Depending on the course offerings, students can complete several certificates to prepare them for a new career or for advancement in their careers as they work toward an associate degree. All 58 North Carolina community colleges offer certificates.

Credential	Credit Hours
Associate in Applied Science (AAS)	64–76 credits
Associate in Arts (AA)	60–61 credits
Associate in Science (AS)	60–61 credits
Associate in Fine Arts (AFA)	64 credits
Associate in General Education (AGE)	64–65 credits
Diploma	36–48 credits
Certificate	12–18 credits

Programs of Study at North Carolina Community Colleges

On the next several pages, you will see most of the specific programs that are available at North Carolina community colleges as of Spring 2014. The programs are degree programs unless otherwise noted. Check your college's website to see which programs are offered at your college.

Agricultural and Natural Resources Technologies

- Agribusiness Technology
- Applied Animal Science Technology
- Aquaculture Technology
- Equine Business Technology
- Equine Training Technology
- Fish and Wildlife Management Technology
- Forest Management Technology
- Golf Course Management Technology
- Golf Equipment Technician (Diploma)
- Greenhouse and Grounds Maintenance (Certificate)
- Horticulture Technology
- Landscape Gardening
- Marine Sciences
- Marine Technology
- Sustainable Agriculture
- Swine Management Technology
- Turfgrass Management Technology
- Viticulture and Enology Technology

Biological and Chemical Technologies

- Agricultural Biotechnology
- Alternative Energy Technology: Biofuels
- Aquarium Science Technology
- Biopharmaceutical Technology
- Biotechnology
- Chemical Technology
- Environmental Management Technology
- Environmental Science Technology
- Invasive Species Management Technology
- Laboratory Technology
- Nanotechnology
- Zoological Science Technology

Business Technologies

- Accounting
- Business Administration
- Business Administration/Banking and Finance
- Business Administration/Customer Service
- Business Administration/Electronic Commerce
- Business Administration/Human Resources Management
- Business Administration/Import Export Compliance
- Business Administration/International Business
- Business Administration/Logistics Management
- Business Administration/Marketing and Retailing
- Business Administration/Operations Management
- Business Administration/Public Administration
- Business Administration/Shooting and Hunting Sports Management
- Computer Information Technology
- Computer Programming
- Computer Technology Integration
- Court Reporting and Captioning
- Database Management
- Data Entry (Certificate)
- Digital Media Technology
- Entertainment Technologies
- Entrepreneurship
- Financial Services
- Gaming Management
- Global Logistics Technology
- Healthcare Business Informatics

- Healthcare Management Technology
- Health Unit Coordinator (Certificate)
- High Performance Computing
- Hospitality Management
- Information Systems Security
- Information Systems Security/Security Hardware
- Insurance (Certificate)
- Medical Office Administration
- Medical Transcription (Diploma)
- Networking Technology
- Nonprofit Leadership and Management
- Office Administration
- Office Administration/Legal
- Office Administration/Virtual Office Assistance
- Paralegal Technology
- Project Management Technology
- Real Estate
- Real Estate Appraisal
- Real Estate Licensing (Certificate)
- Simulation and Game Development
- Travel and Tourism Technology
- Voice Writing Realtime Reporting
- Web Technologies

Commercial and Artistic Production Technologies

- Advertising and Graphic Design
- Broadcasting and Production Technology
- Digital Effects and Animation Technology
- Film and Video Production Technology
- Fine and Creative Woodworking
- Graphic Arts and Imaging Technology
- Graphic Arts and Imaging Technology/ Flexography
- Gunsmithing
- Gunsmithing (diploma)
- Interior Design
- Metal Engraving (diploma)
- Photographic Technology
- Photographic Technology/ Biocommunications Photography
- Photographic Technology/Commercial Photography
- Photographic Technology/ Photojournalism
- Photographic Technology/Portrait Studio Management

- Professional Arts and Crafts: Sculpture
- Professional Crafts: Clay
- Professional Crafts: Fiber
- Professional Crafts: Jewelry
- Professional Crafts: Wood
- Taxidermy (Diploma)

Construction Technologies

- Air Conditioning, Heating, and Refrigeration Technology
- Boat Building (Diploma)
- Building Construction Technology
- Cabinetmaking (Diploma)
- Carpentry (Diploma)
- Commercial Refrigeration Technology
- Construction Management Technology
- Electric Line Construction Technology
- Electrical Systems Technology
- Heavy Equipment Operator (Diploma)
- Historic Preservation Technology
- Masonry (Diploma)
- Plumbing (Diploma)

Engineering Technologies

- Applied Engineering Technology
- Architectural Technology
- Automation Engineering Technology
- Civil Engineering Technology
- Computer Engineering Technology
- Electrical Engineering Technology
- Electronics Engineering Technology
- Environmental Engineering Technology
- Geomatics Technology
- Geospatial Mapping Technology
- Geospatial Technology
- Industrial Engineering Technology
- Landscape Architecture Technology
- Laser and Photonics Technology
- Low Impact Development
- Mechanical Engineering Technology
- Mechatronics Engineering Technology
- Sustainability Technologies
- Telecommunications and Network Engineering Technology

Health Sciences

- Associate Degree Nursing
- Cancer Information Management
- Cardiovascular/Vascular Interventional Technology (Diploma)
- Cardiovascular Sonography

- Cardiovascular Technology (Invasive and Non-Invasive)
- Central Sterile Processing (Certificate)
- Clinical Trials Research Associate
- Computed Tomography & Magnetic Resonance Imaging Technology (Diploma)
- Cytotechnology (Certificate)
- Dental Assisting (Diploma)
- Dental Hygiene
- Dental Laboratory Technology
- Dialysis Technology (Diploma)
- Dietetic Technician
- Electroneurodiagnostic Technology
- Emergency Medical Science
- Health and Fitness Science
- Health Care Technology (Certificate)
- Health Information Technology
- Healthcare Interpreting
- Histotechnology
- Human Services Technology
- Human Services Technology/Animal Assisted Interactions
- Human Services Technology/ Developmental Disabilities
- Human Services Technology/ Gerontology
- Human Services Technology/Mental Health
- Human Services Technology/Social Services
- Human Services Technology/Substance Abuse
- Interventional Cardiac and Vascular Technology
- Licensed Practical Nurse Refresher (Certificate)
- Magnetic Resonance Imaging
- Medical Assisting
- Medical Dosimetry (Diploma)
- Medical Laboratory Technology
- Medical Sonography
- Nuclear Medicine Technology
- Nursing Assistant (Certificate)
- Occupational Therapy Assistant
- Ophthalmic Medical Assistant (Diploma)
- Optical Apprentice (Certificate)
- Optical Laboratory Mechanics (Certificate)

- Opticianry
- Pharmacy Technology
- Phlebotomy (Certificate)
- Physical Therapist Assistant (2-year program)
- Physical Therapist Assistant (1+1)
- Polysomnography
- Positron Emission Tomography (Diploma)
- Practical Nursing (Diploma)
- Radiation Therapy Technology
- Radiography
- Respiratory Therapy
- Speech-Language Pathology Assistant
- Surgical Technology
- Therapeutic Massage
- Therapeutic Recreation Assistant
- Veterinary Medical Technology

Industrial Technologies

- Aerostructure Manufacturing and Repair
- Biomedical Equipment Technology
- Bioprocess Technology
- Computer-Aided Drafting Technology
- Computer-Integrated Machining
- Electric Utility Substation and Relay Technology
- Electrical Power Production Technology
- Environment, Health, and Safety Technology
- Facility Maintenance Technology
- Facility Maintenance Worker (Diploma)
- Furniture Production Technology
- Furniture Production Technology/ Design and Product Development
- Furniture Upholstery (Diploma)
- Industrial Management Technology
- Industrial Systems Technology
- Manufacturing Technology
- Mechanical Drafting Technology
- Nondestructive Examination Technology
- Nuclear Technology
- Pulp and Paper Technology
- Quality Assurance and Continuous Improvement
- Telecommunications Installation and Maintenance (Diploma)
- Welding Technology

Public Service Technologies
- Animal Care and Management Technology
- Baking and Pastry Arts
- Barbering
- Basic Law Enforcement Training (Certificate)
- Community Spanish Interpreter
- Cosmetology
- Cosmetology Instructor (Certificate)
- Criminal Justice Technology
- Criminal Justice Technology/Financial Crime/Computer Fraud
- Criminal Justice Technology/Latent Evidence
- Culinary Arts
- Cyber Crime Technology
- Early Childhood Education
- Emergency Preparedness Technology
- Esthetics Instructor (Certificate)
- Esthetics Technology
- Fire Protection Technology
- Food Service Technology (Diploma)
- Funeral Service Education
- General Occupational Technology
- Infant/Toddler Care (Certificate)
- Interpreter Education
- Lateral Entry (Certificate)
- Library and Information Technology
- Manicuring Instructor (Certificate)
- Manicuring/Nail Technology (Certificate)
- Occupational Education Associate
- Outdoor Leadership
- Recreation and Leisure Studies
- Resort and Spa Management
- School-Age Care (Certificate)
- School Age Education

Transport Systems Technologies
- Agricultural Systems Technology
- Automotive Customizing Technology
- Automotive Management
- Automotive Restoration Technology (Diploma)
- Automotive Systems Technology
- Automotive Systems Technology/Race Car Performance
- Aviation Electronics (Avionics) Technology
- Aviation Management and Career Pilot Technology
- Aviation Systems Technology
- Boat Manufacture and Service (Diploma)
- Collision Repair and Refinishing Technology
- Diesel and Heavy Equipment Technology
- Construction Equipment Systems Technology
- Marine Propulsion Systems (Diploma)
- Motorcycle Mechanics (Diploma)
- Motorsports Management Technology
- Race Car Technology
- Recreational Vehicle Maintenance and Repair Technology
- Small Engine and Equipment Repair (Diploma)
- Truck Driver Training (Certificate)

Plans of Study

When you are admitted to a specific degree, diploma, or certificate program, you will use that program's **Plan of Study** document to know what courses are required for a credential. Depending on what community college you are attending, your Plan of Study may be called Course Hour Requirements, Curriculum, Curriculum Standards, Checksheet, Degree Plan, Course Requirements, or Individual Graduation Plan.

The Plan of Study typically includes the required general education and major courses. Be sure to follow the Plan of Study for the year in which you were admitted to your program. For example, if you were admitted in 2014–2015, then you should use the 2014–2015 Plan of Study, not the 2013–2014 Plan of Study.

You may be required to take additional courses as pre-requisites or co-requisites to the courses required of your Plan of Study. These pre-requisite courses are typically listed at the bottom of the Plan of Study.

A **pre-requisite course** is one that you must successfully complete before enrolling in a higher level course. For example, students must take and pass BIO 168 (Anatomy and Physiology I) before they can take BIO 169 (Anatomy and Physiology II). BIO 168 is a pre-requisite for BIO 169.

Common pre-requisites are **developmental education** courses. These are English and reading and math classes that prepare students for success in college-level courses. Developmental education classes have course numbers under 100, like DRE 097. If your placement test results indicate that you need any developmental education courses, then you are required to take and pass them (sometimes with a B or higher and sometimes with a grade of P for Pass), but the developmental education credit hours do not count toward the total number of credits required by your Plan of Study. For example, if you place into developmental education courses and you plan to earn the 60–61 credits required for the AS degree, then you may actually have to complete 66 or 70 or 73 credits depending on how many developmental education classes you need. The grades you earn in developmental education classes may count toward your cumulative GPA and will probably count toward your Satisfactory Academic Progress if you are receiving financial aid (see Chapter 10 for more information about GPAs and Chapter 11 for more information about financial aid).

Some students also have to take **English as a Foreign Language** (EFL) courses as pre-requisites for their programs. If your first language is not English, then you may be required to take an additional placement test that may indicate that you need EFL courses to prepare you for the academic language skills you will need to be successful in college. Like developmental education courses, EFL courses do not count toward the required number of credits for your Program of Study, but your grades in EFL courses may count toward your cumulative GPA.

A **co-requisite course** is one that you must complete at the same time as a required course. For example, at some colleges, PHY 110 (Conceptual Physics) and PHY 110A (Conceptual Physics Lab) must be taken in the same semester. PHY 110 and PHY 110A are co-requisites at those colleges.

Plans of Study are frequently organized to list non-developmental education pre-requisites before additional requirements and to list co-requisites in the same semester. Also, your advisor can help you plan your schedule to take into consideration any pre-requisites or co-requisites.

Your semester-by-semester class schedule will probably not look exactly like your program's Plan of Study because of any combination of the following reasons:

- You may have to first complete pre-requisites, like developmental education courses.

- You may take fewer courses than are listed in a single semester on the Plan of Study.

- You may enter your program in a different semester than the first one listed on the Plan of Study.

In addition to paying attention to pre-requisites and co-requisites as you read your Plan of Study, consider credit hours and contact hours.

Credit hours are the number of hours associated with a particular class. Each Plan of Study requires a certain number of credit hours. The credit hours are used to calculate your GPA and determine your tuition bill each semester.

Contact hours, on the other hand, are the number of hours you spend in class each week. For example, CIS 110 (Introduction to Computers) is three credit hours and four contact hours. If you take CIS 110, then you'll receive three credits on your transcript, and you'll be billed for three credits. But you'll actually spend four hours in class each week.

Look for credit hours and contact hours on most Plans of Study. You will often have to add the "class hours," "lab hours," and "clinical hours" on the Plan of Study to determine the number of contact hours. If you can't find the credit hours and contact hours on your Plan of Study, then you can look up the contact hours associated with each of your classes on your college's website.

Now is a good time to look for your Plan of Study at your college. Most colleges post Plans of Study on their website. And most Plans of Study include the details described in this chapter. Look specifically for credit hours and contact hours. Look also for the organization. For example, is the Plan of Study in chronological order (first semester, second semester, etc.)? Or is the Plan of Study organized by discipline (required Natural Sciences courses, required Humanities/Fine Arts courses, etc.). Typically, university transfer Plans of Study (Associate in Arts, Associate in Science, and Associate in Fine Arts) are not in chronological order, and they include lots of choices for students to make about exact courses. Therefore, the information about Major Pathways, Pre-Majors, and Study Tracks in the next section is very important for university transfer students.

● University Transfer Major Pathways

University transfer Plans of Study typically list disciplines or categories of courses that are required for the degree. Within these disciplines, there may be several courses listed that students can select from. University transfer students have a lot of choices to make. Therefore, in addition to choosing to pursue the AA or AS degree, university transfer students should also select a Major Pathway, Pre-Major, or Study Track. These documents list which specific classes are preferred for a specific major and/or a specific university.

Historically, transfer students have used Pre-Majors and Study Tracks to select the most useful community college courses. **Pre-Majors** are lists of courses recommended by North Carolina community college and university faculty to prepare students for a specific major at the senior institution. **Study Tracks** are also lists of recommended courses, but they are developed by community college faculty, typically for specific senior institutions.

Under the recently revised Comprehensive Articulation Agreement, a new resource is being developed for community college transfer students. **Major Pathways** are lists of courses recommended by North Carolina public universities to prepare transfer students for success in specific majors at the universities. Universities develop the Major Pathways to best prepare students for success upon transfer to the senior institutions.

Universities began to develop the Major Pathways in Spring 2014. The first Major Pathways included the following most popular transfer majors:

Arts	Science
• Business Administration • Communications • Criminal Justice • Elementary Education • English • History • Middle Grades Education • Political Science • Psychology • Social Work	• Biology

For the most up-to-date list of Major Pathways, check the UNC General Administration website at www.northcarolina.edu.

As the Major Pathways are created and integrated into the advising practices at the community college, students may be directed to one of the three resources described in this section (Major Pathways, Pre-Majors, or Study Tracks) depending on when they are admitted to the community college. Check you college's website or college catalog for information about what resources are available to transfer students at your college.

Now is a good time to research the various AA and AS Major Pathways, Pre-Majors, and Study Tracks that are available at your college. As you review these documents, notice that the recommended coursework is different, especially in Natural Sciences and Mathematics. Also notice that the credit hours may be listed as SHC ("Semester Hours Credit") but that the contact hours may not be listed. You can always look up the contact hours for specific courses on your college's website.

See your college's website or speak to an advisor about what Major Pathways, Pre-Majors, and Study Tracks are most appropriate for students at your college.

Three Options for Transfer to Senior Institutions

As you explore your academic goals, you'll need clarification about your transfer options. There are several options, and you should weigh the strengths and weaknesses of each to determine which option is best for you. No matter what associate degree you pursue at your community college—AA, AS, AFA, or AAS—you have the opportunity to transfer your classes and your degree to a senior institution. The three paths to transfer also offer lots of choices in terms of how quickly students can transfer and how easily their community college classes will transfer.

Option 1: No Degree

Some students take just a few classes at the community college and then transfer to a senior institution. As long as you are taking classes that are transferable and that are college-level and you earn a C or better in your classes, then you can transfer whenever you are accepted to the senior institution, and the Comprehensive Articulation Agreement (CAA) will protect your classes.

The **Comprehensive Articulation Agreement** is a North Carolina law that states that all community college courses that are designated as transferable will transfer to all public North Carolina universities and to private colleges that have signed on to the agreement. The CAA protects transfer to all public North Carolina universities to help students have a seamless transfer experience. Many private colleges have also chosen to follow the CAA, but not all of them. Private institutions that agree to follow the provisions of the CAA sign on with the ICAA, the Independent Comprehensive Articulation Agreement. If you plan to transfer to a private university, then you should make sure that the university will accept the classes you take at the community college. Please note that the CAA was revised in February 2014; the information that follows represents the changes that were approved at that time.

The recently revised CAA classifies transferable courses in three categories: **Universal General Education Transfer Component (UGETC) courses**, **general education**, and **pre-major/elective courses**. UGETC designated courses are guaranteed to transfer and to be applied toward the senior institution's lower-division general education course requirements. General education and pre-major/elective courses are also guaranteed to transfer, but the senior institution can decide whether the course will count as part of general education or elective credit if the transfer student does not graduate with an AA or AS degree prior to transfer. UGETC courses that you take at the community college can count as general education courses and pre-major/electives, but pre-major/elective courses cannot count as general education courses.

Tips for a Seamless Transfer

- Earn a C or better in your classes. The Comprehensive Articulation Agreement won't protect your transfer classes if you don't have a grade of C or better.

- Do your homework. University websites have lots of information about transfer admissions. Many universities state exactly which classes they want transfer students to bring to the university.

- Use your college's resources. Look for advising and transfer centers on your campus to help you better understand the CAA and find out which Bilateral Articulation Agreements you are eligible for.

Students who plan to transfer before they earn an associate degree are limited to transferring the following number of UGETC credits:

Discipline	Maximum Number of Credits Community College Students Can Transfer without the AA or AS Degree
English Composition	6 credit hours
Humanities/Fine Arts/Communications	9 credit hours
Social/Behavioral Sciences	9 credit hours
Mathematics	8 credit hours
Natural Sciences	8 credit hours

If you earn this many transferable credits at a community college, then it is in your best interest to complete the associate degree before you transfer. See Option 2 for transfer for the benefits of earning the AA or AS degree.

You can always look at the community college course description to find out if a particular course is transferable. And if you do not plan to earn a degree before you transfer, then it is critical that you look for and accurately interpret the transfer statements on the course descriptions. For example, ENG 111 (Wrting and Inquiry) is a transferable UGETC course. (The details in the table below are from the Combined Course Library resource on the North Carolina Community College System website.) You can tell that ENG 111 is a transferable general education core course because the last sentences of the course description say so. This means that ENG 111 will transfer, and it will count toward the English composition requirement at the university.

ENG 111   Writing and Inquiry

Class 3 Lab 0 Clinical 0 Work 0
Credit 3

This course is designed to develop the ability to produce clear writing in a variety of genres and formats using a recursive process. Emphasis includes inquiry, analysis, effective use of rhetorical strategies, thesis development, audience awareness, and revision. Upon completion, students should be able to produce unified, coherent, well-developed essays using standard written English.

Minimum State Pre-requisites
DRE 098

Minimum State Co-requisites
None

College Transfer
This course has been approved for transfer under the CAA as a general education course in English Composition.
This course has been approved for transfer under the ICAA as a general education course in English Composition.
This is a Universal General Education Transfer Component (UGETC) course.

Contrast the course description for ENG 111 with the course description for ENG 273 below. African-American Literature is also a transferable course, and it is protected by the Comprehensive Articulation Agreement to be guaranteed to transfer. But it will not count toward your English composition requirement. It will transfer as a pre-major/elective course only.

ENG 273   African American Literature

Class 3 Lab 0 Clinical 0 Work 0
Credit 3

This course provides a survey of the development of African-American literature from its beginnings to the present. Emphasis is placed on historical and cultural context, themes, literary traditions, and backgrounds of the authors. Upon completion, students should be able to interpret, analyze, and respond to selected texts.

Minimum State Pre-requisites
ENG-112, ENG-113, or ENG-114

Minimum State Co-requisites
None

College Transfer
This course has been approved for transfer under the CAA as a premajor and/or elective course requirement.
This course has been approved for transfer under the ICAA as a premajor and/or elective course requirement.

Finally, some community college courses are not transferable at all. The course description for DRE 098 doesn't say anything about the Comprehensive Articulation Agreement or the transferability of the course. That's because DRE 098 is not a transferable course. It will not transfer to any university.

DRE 098   Integrated Reading and Writing III

Class 2.5 Lab 1 Clinical 0 Work 0
Credit 3

This course is designed to develop proficiency in integrated and contextualized reading and writing skills and strategies. Topics include reading and writing processes, critical thinking strategies, and recognition and composition of well-developed, coherent, and unified texts; these topics are taught using texts primarily in the Lexile™ range of 1185 to 1385. Upon completion, students should be able to apply those skills toward understanding a variety of texts at the career and college ready level and toward composing a documented essay. Note: TM represents registered trademark.

Minimum State Pre-requisites
DRE 097

Minimum State Co-requisites
None

College Transfer
N/A

We also know that DRE 098 is not a transferable course because the course number is less than 100. Any course that has a course number less than 100 will not transfer. For example, DRE 096 and BIO 092 will not transfer.

Students who transfer before they complete an associate degree will have their transcripts evaluated course by course by the senior institution admissions office. The university will decide how the transferable credits transfer, for example as general education or pre-major/elective courses. If you do not complete an AA or AS degree, then you will be required to take additional general education courses at the university in order to fulfill the university's general education requirements.

Option 2: The AA and AS Degrees

The Comprehensive Articulation Agreement offers students who complete an Associate in Arts or Associate in Science degree at a community college considerably better protection than students who don't earn a degree before they transfer.

All North Carolina community colleges offer Associate in Arts (AA) degrees, and most offer Associate in Science (AS) degrees. The AA and AS degrees require a minimum of 30 credit hours of UGETC designated courses and additional general education and pre-major/elective courses. The AA and AS degree programs require 60–61 credit hours total. The CAA requires that transfer students earn a grade of C or better in their transfer courses and an overall GPA of 2.0. See your Plan of Study and Major Pathway/Pre-Major/Study Track for a list of the courses required for these degrees at your community college.

There are five significant benefits to earning the AA or AS degree before you transfer.

The first benefit of earning an AA or AS degree before you transfer is that all 60–61 credit hours will transfer as a package when you are accepted to the university. That is, all of the courses within the degree program will transfer together. And you will have fewer classes to take at the university than if you transfer before completing the AA or AS degree because you will be given academic credit for more classes from the community college. Bachelor degree programs typically require 120 credit hours; by completing the AA or AS degree, you are halfway finished with the requirements for the bachelor degree. The recently revised CAA recommends that students identify their major and the senior institution that they plan to transfer to before completing 30 credit hours. That way, you have plenty of time to take the courses that are preferred by both the major and the senior institution you choose.

Secondly, the AA and AS degrees include the maximum UGETC designated courses that you can complete at the community college, so when you are accepted to the university, you will have fulfilled the university's lower-division general education core requirements. You will not have to take additional lower-division general education courses. However, do be advised that there may be additional university courses required of you beyond the lower-division general education core courses depending on the requirements of individual majors and senior institutions. The CAA prevents universities from requiring transfer students to take courses or fulfill university expectations that they do not require of their native students. However, there may be university requirements that native students fulfill in their freshman or sophomore years that you will have to fulfill later.

Thirdly, you will transfer as a junior. You will be able to move even more quickly into your major electives and toward graduation with a bachelor's degree. You'll also be eligible for the privileges that students with junior status receive, for example, early registration and preferred parking on campus.

Fourthly, completion of the AA or AS degree satisfies the University of North Carolina **Minimum Admission Requirements (MAR)** and **Minimum Course Requirements (MCR)**. The MAR include specific standards for high school GPA and ACT or SAT test scores. When you earn the AA or AS degree, you do not have to submit your high school GPA or ACT/SAT test scores to the university. The MCR specify the number of high school

units students must have completed to be considered for admission to the university. If your high school transcript does not include all of the courses required by the MCR, then you may not be considered for admission to the senior institution without the AA or AS degree.

Finally, you can take advantage of the **Transfer Assured Admissions Policy (TAAP)**, which states that students who earn the AA or AS degree are guaranteed admission to one university in the UNC system, though not necessarily to the school of the student's choice. To qualify for TAAP, you must earn an AA or AS degree from a North Carolina community college, pass all of your transferable classes with a C or better, and have a cumulative GPA of 2.0 or higher. And you must be in good standing and eligible to return to the school you are transferring from. If you are not admitted to the university or universities that you apply to, then you should visit the College Foundation of North Carolina (CFNC) website to find out how to take advantage of the Transfer Assured Admissions Policy.

Again, the purpose of the CAA is to improve the transfer of credits from North Carolina community colleges to the University of North Carolina system schools. If upon transfer you think that the terms of the CAA were not honored, then you have the right to use the **Transfer Credit Appeal Procedure** to present your argument. Look for a link to the Transfer Credit Appeal Procedure on your college website or on the North Carolina Community College System website.

Option 3: The AAS and AFA Degrees

The first two options for transfer focused on students' rights and responsibilities under the Comprehensive Articulation Agreement. North Carolina community colleges also offer Associate in Applied Science (AAS) degrees, which prepare students to enter careers immediately after graduation, and Associate in Fine Arts (AFA) degrees, which prepare students for additional study of specific fine arts, including music, art, and drama. AAS degrees are not designed for transfer. Individual community colleges can offer dozens of these degrees, including Paralegal Technology, Nursing, Networking Technologies, Agricultural Biotechnology, Occupational Therapy Assistant, and Automotive Technology. However, many students who complete AAS degrees find that they want to continue their education with a bachelor's degree. It is critical that these students understand the protections granted to them as community college students. Unlike AAS degrees, AFA degrees are designed to transfer but only into very specific majors at specific senior institutions. The AFA degree requires considerably fewer general education courses and more major courses.

The Comprehensive Articulation Agreement (CAA) does not protect AAS or AFA degrees the same way it protects AA or AS degrees.

All Associate in Applied Science and Associate in Fine Arts degrees require some Universal General Education Transfer Component designated courses, and these courses are transferable and protected by the CAA. For example, ENG 111 (Writing and Inquiry), PSY 150 (General Psychology), and COM 231 (Public Speaking) are listed on many AAS and AFA Plans of Study. These individual UGETC courses would transfer to the university and count towards the university's required lower-division general education requirements.

The AAS and AFA Plans of Study also include specific program or major courses. Most of these courses are not designed for transfer to all universities and similarly are not protected by the Comprehensive Articulation Agreement. If you are unsure of whether your courses are designed for transfer, look for the course description.

Although the CAA doesn't apply to many AAS and AFA courses, students can frequently transfer their AAS and AFA degrees to senior institutions through Bilateral Articulation Agreements, which allow AAS and AFA students to transfer their entire degrees to a university. **Bilateral Articulation Agreements** are transfer agreements between a specific university and a specific community college. They are for specific degree programs. For example, Cape Fear Community College and UNC–Greensboro have a Bilateral Articulation Agreement to help students who graduate from Cape Fear with an AAS degree in Radiography transfer to UNC–Greensboro to earn a bachelor's degree in Radiography. Similarly, Stanly Community College and Winston-Salem State University have a Bilateral Articulation Agreement for students who earn an AAS degree in Accounting.

AAS and AFA degree students should look to their community college's website and/or college catalog for an up-to-date list of Bilateral Articulation Agreements that are available to them.

The Venn diagram that follows represents the similarities and differences between the Comprehensive Articulation Agreement and Bilateral Articulation Agreements. You can see the unique features of the CAA in the left circle and the unique features of the Bilateral Articulation Agreements in the right circle. Where the circles overlap, you can see what the CAA and Bilateral Articulation Agreements have in common.

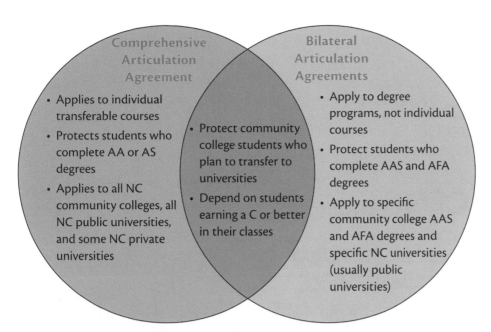

Comprehensive Articulation Agreement

- Applies to individual transferable courses
- Protects students who complete AA or AS degrees
- Applies to all NC community colleges, all NC public universities, and some NC private universities

(intersection)
- Protect community college students who plan to transfer to universities
- Depend on students earning a C or better in their classes

Bilateral Articulation Agreements

- Apply to degree programs, not individual courses
- Protect students who complete AAS and AFA degrees
- Apply to specific community college AAS and AFA degrees and specific NC universities (usually public universities)

In addition to deciding how to transfer to a university, community college students need to decide early where to transfer. Fortunately, there are many resources available to help you decide which senior institution is right for you. University websites often have webpages specific to transfer admissions. Also, college recruiters often visit community college campuses, and they can be a great resource for information about the university.

Finally, the College Foundation of North Carolina website is another useful resource in academic goal exploration. See the screenshot and information that follows to learn more about how to use CFNC for academic goal exploration.

STUDENT NOTES

CFNC: Plan for College

The online CFNC planning tool is an excellent resource for self-assessment (as you learned in Chapter 1). It is also a very useful research tool for academic goal exploration.

When you log in to CFNC, move your cursor on the "Plan" tab and click on "For College."

See page 14 for a step-by-step guide to creating a CFNC account. If you already have an account, then click on the "Log on to My CFNC" to access your account and bypass the account creation process.

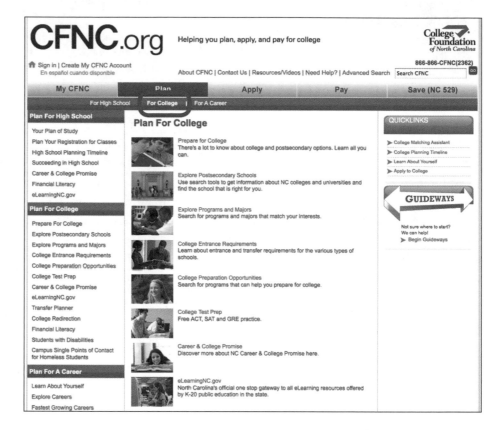

On this page, there are additional resources that will help with your academic goal exploration. Look for the "Explore Postsecondary Schools" and "Explore Programs and Majors" links on the left to research what careers your academic program will prepare you for. This is also a great resource to find out what additional credentials may be required to advance in your field. CFNC is a North Carolina-specific tool, and the connections it makes between academics and careers are incredibly valuable to North Carolina residents.

You can also search North Carolina public and private colleges and universities (including community colleges) by name, major, alphabetical listings, locations, and other search parameters. You can even incorporate the results of the Interest Profiler and Work Values Sorter (see page 18 for more details) into your search for a major if you are undecided about your major.

Conclusion

Successful community college students understand not only the specific requirements for their chosen program of study, but also how their program fits within the larger community college structure. As you have likely noticed by now, community college students are very diverse in age, and you may return to the community college in the future to pursue a different credential. After studying the concepts in Chapter 2 and applying them to your own Plan of Study and/or Major Pathway/Pre-Major/Study Track, you are well prepared to make realistic decisions about your academic future. You are also ready to look toward your career options, as you'll see in Chapter 3.

If you haven't recorded your program of study or your Major Pathway/Pre-Major/Study Track on page 3, do so now for easy reference.

CHAPTER 2
Academic Goal Exploration

1. Match the community college credentials with their definitions.

___ Certificate

___ Diploma

___ Associate in Arts

___ Associate in Science

___ Associate in General Education

___ Associate in Applied Science

___ Associate in Fine Arts

a. a degree (64 credit hours) designed for individuals wishing to broaden their education, with emphasis on personal interest, growth, and development

b. a degree (60–61 credit hours) with an emphasis on courses such as English, fine arts, foreign languages, history, philosophy, psychology, or sociology

c. a degree (64–76 credit hours) that prepares students for a particular career

d. a credential requiring a shorter time commitment from students, specifically 12–18 credit hours

e. a degree (60–61 credit hours) with an emphasis on courses such as biology, chemistry, engineering, geology, mathematics, or physics

f. a degree (64 credit hours) with an emphasis on courses such as art, drama, or music

g. a credential requiring a shorter time commitment from students, specifically 36–48 credit hours

2. Identify at least one advantage and one disadvantage of the three options for transfer to a university.

Option 1: No Degree

Advantages	Disadvantages

Option 2: The AA and AS Degrees

Advantages	Disadvantages

Option 3: The AAS and AFA Degrees

Advantages	Disadvantages

Career Goal Exploration

I n addition to researching what academic options you have at your community college and beyond, you should also consider your career options. You can use the career goal exploration resources in this chapter to find the careers that best suit the personality, interests, and values you identified through the various self-assessment tools in Chapter 1. As you learned in Chapter 1, individuals whose personality, interests, and values match their careers can expect to experience a high level of job satisfaction from their careers. Use the resources described in this chapter to identify careers that suit your personal characteristics.

As you move through the career goal exploration process, be mindful of what you learned about your academic goals, too. Different college credentials prepare you for different careers. When you research a specific career, pay careful attention to the education and training required to enter that career. You may find that you already have the necessary education, or you may discover that you will need several credentials beyond the associate degree in order to enter the career.

Chapter 3 will address the following very useful tools in career goal exploration:

- Occupational Outlook Handbook,
- College Foundation of North Carolina (CFNC),
- Other online resources,
- Informational interviews, and
- Job shadowing.

Occupational Outlook Handbook

The **Occupational Outlook Handbook** is published every two years by the United States Department of Labor's Bureau of Labor Statistics. It is a reliable source of information about a wide variety of careers across the United States. Specifically, you can use the Occupational Outlook Handbook to research a career's daily job tasks, starting and average salaries, projections about the growth of the career, related fields, and links to professional organizations and other useful online resources.

You can find a hard copy of the Occupational Outlook Handbook in many libraries, including many community college campus libraries. You can also use the Occupational Outlook Handbook online at http://www.bls.gov/ooh/. See the following screenshots to learn how to use this very useful online tool for career exploration.

When you open the Occupational Outlook Handbook online, look for the search field "Search Handbook" in the right-hand corner of the page. Type the career that you want to explore in the search field.

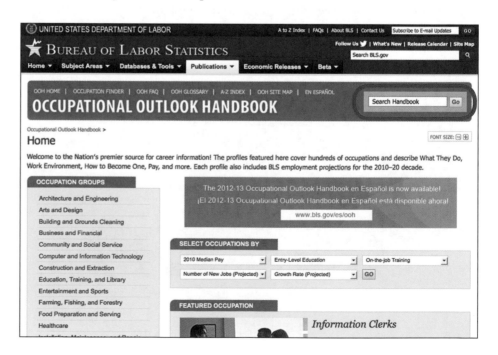

The screenshot below shows the result of a search for "respiratory therapist." On the results page, you can find useful information about respiratory therapists. Notice the tabs at the top of the page that identify the content available on this specific career. Specifically, look for "What They Do," "Work Environment," "How to Become One," "Pay," "Job Outlook," "Similar Occupations," and "Contacts for More Info."

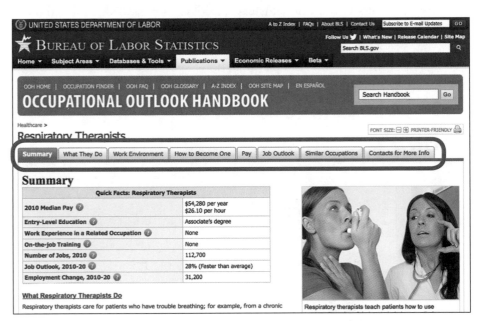

Depending on your search terms, you may have to find your career in a results list. For example, if you type "nurse" in the BLS search engine, then you'll get a results page with links to resources for "registered nurses," "licensed practical and vocational nurses," "nursing and psychiatric aides," and so on. Click on the result that matches your personal career goal.

Note, too, the URL for the links on the search results page, and select links with "ooh" in the web address. The code "ooh" refers to the Occupational Outlook Handbook. If you choose a web address without "ooh" in it, then you may find yourself looking at Occupational Employment Statistics (which are helpful, but not the full picture) or resources for K–12 students (which are also helpful, but not as thorough as the Occupational Outlook Handbook).

Likewise, you may need to use different search terms to find your career choice. For example, students in the AAS Early Childhood Education program should search for "Child Care Workers" if that is the career they plan to begin. AA students who plan to major in psychology at a senior institution would use the search terms "Psychologist," "Psychiatrist," or "Guidance Counselor," depending on which career they specifically plan to enter (and depending on how many credentials they are planning to earn).

CFNC: Plan for a Career

You learned about the CFNC website in Chapter 1 as a resource for self-assessments and in Chapter 2 in the discussion of academic goal exploration. This site is also a very useful tool in career goal exploration.

Log in to CFNC and click on the orange "Plan" tab and then "For A Career" to research careers by job title, clusters (or fields such as "Education and Training"), or even based on your personal results on the Interest Profiler and Work Values Sorter. As you read your search results, keep in mind that the salary information, job outlook projections, etc., in CFNC are specific to North Carolina whereas the Occupational Outlook Handbook lists national averages.

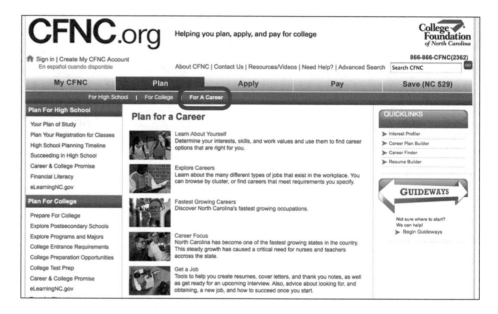

Two other useful links on the "Plan for a Career" page include "Compare Careers," which will help you compare and contrast two careers side by side. You can compare the characteristics of two careers, including the job tasks, work hours, average starting salaries, and physical demands.

Finally, be sure to look at the "Video List" under "Find Careers By" at the bottom of the page. The "Video List" link takes you to video clips of professionals in various careers. The videos can help you visualize how you might use the skills and knowledge you are learning in the classroom, lab, and/or clinical setting.

Plan to spend the time necessary getting familiar with the CFNC website, so you can take advantage of this incredibly rich source of information on North Carolina education and career opportunities.

Other Online Resources

The Occupational Outlook Handbook and CFNC are only two of hundreds of websites that can be useful in the career goal exploration stage of goal discernment. Look for websites that offer more than salary information; useful career goal exploration sites are comprehensive, like the Occupational Outlook Handbook and CFNC. As you look for additional online resources, think critically about what makes a website good. Four general criteria for website analysis include:

Accuracy

A reliable website contains information that is correct. The website is updated regularly and verified by a trustworthy source. The website is also proofread carefully for spelling and grammar errors.

Authority

A reliable website is also sponsored by a knowledgeable author or agency. Look at the domain at the end of the URL for information about the website sponsor. For example, a .com website is a commercial site and often exists for the sole reason of selling a product. A .edu website, on the other hand, is published by an educational organization, and a .org website is published by a nonprofit organization. These are websites that exist to provide information, not to sell you a product.

Objectivity

A reliable website may or may not be designed to persuade viewers. If the site is trying to persuade viewers, consider the message carefully. Look specifically for the quantity and types of advertisements on the page for insights into its objectivity.

Currency

A reliable website is kept up to date. Look for information at the top or bottom of the page about when the website was published or last updated. Avoid websites that reference information that is several years out of date. As you know, many career fields are dynamic and the education required for a specific career as well as the average starting salary can change in a span of just a few years.

The following types of websites most often meet these criteria:

- College and university websites

- Links on college and university websites specific to majors and departments

- Academic and professional organizations

- Websites for companies you may want to work for

- Links on your community college's website to your chosen department or Program of Study

- Links from the Occupational Outlook Handbook or CFNC websites

STUDENT NOTES

Two career goal exploration websites that consistently meet these criteria are the O*NET OnLine website (http://www.onetonline.org/) and the North Carolina Career Resource Network SOICC (www.ncsoicc.org). Both websites use the language of the Holland Codes and work values to sort careers and match individuals with appropriate careers. Also, the websites provide trustworthy information about the following aspects of individual careers: job descriptions, typical job responsibilities, required skills and abilities, average salaries, and projected growth.

Consider exploring the O*NET and SOICC websites if the College Foundation of North Carolina and Occupational Outlook Handbook websites provide you with insufficient information about careers that interest you.

Informational Interviews

Keep in mind that the informational interview gives you one person's opinion. If you catch someone on a bad day or if you interview someone who dislikes her job, then you may get a very negative opinion.

If this happens to you, consider interviewing a second person, so you'll have two perspectives to compare and contrast.

In addition to your online research, you can also gather valuable information about your future career from other people. In an **informational interview**, you interview someone who is working in the career, company, or industry that interests you, so you can learn more about the career, company, or industry. Conduct an informational interview after you've done some research on your own, so you can ask any questions that you've thought of as a result of your research. Use the guidelines below to get the most out of an informational interview.

Before the Interview

Figure out what you want to get out of the interview. Are you interested in learning about a specific job, trends in the industry, or your interview subject's personal experiences? Use the following categories and questions to guide your preparation for the interview.

Questions about the Job

- Describe what you do on a typical day at work.
- What kind of schedule do you typically work?
- What is the most difficult part of your job?
- Where does your job fit in your company's staffing chart? What are the entry-level positions or more advanced positions?

Questions about the Company

- What opportunities for advancement exist at this company?
- What is the average length of time that people stay with this company?
- What is the culture of this company? (for example, collaborative, competitive, individualistic, supportive)
- Is the company growing now? Is the number of employees growing or shrinking?

Questions about the Individual

- How long have you been working in this career?
- What is your favorite part about your career?
- What do you wish you had known about your career before you started working?
- How well did your educational program prepare you for your career?

Questions about the Industry

- What opportunities for advancement exist in your career?
- How is technology changing the career?
- How frequently do people move in and out of this industry?
- What work-related values are most important for this field? (for example, achievement, recognition, relationships, support)

Questions about You

- What advice do you have for someone who wants to begin working in your career field?
- How well do you think I would fit in at your company?
- What kind of position will my degree/diploma/certificate prepare me for?
- In addition to earning my degree/diploma/certificate, what else should I do to prepare for this career? (for example, volunteering, internships, learning a second language)

To set up the interview, email or call the person that you want to interview. To help you appear to be the serious college student that you are, use professional language. Avoid text-messaging lingo and inappropriate slang. Also, be polite. Say "please" and "thank you," to indicate your respect. Finally, provide flexibility. Don't expect your interview subject to meet with you immediately. You may have to offer a few dates or times to meet if your schedules are very different.

During the Interview

Arrive early to the appointed location of the interview. Start by introducing yourself if you don't already know your interview subject. Tell the person a little bit about yourself, including what you are hoping to learn from the informational interview.

Bring up to 12 questions for a 30–45 minute interview, but prioritize the questions in case the discussion runs long, and you don't have time to ask all of your questions. During the interview either record the conversation (with the interview subject's permission) or take lots of notes.

Finally, be mindful of your interview subject's time. For example, if you have arranged for a 30-minute conversation, then keep an eye on your watch and thank the person for her time at the end of 30 minutes. Ask for her email address or phone number in case you have follow-up questions.

After the Interview

Transcribe your recording of the informational interview or review your notes as soon as possible, so you can fill in any holes in the conversation based on your memory. If you find any gaps in your notes or understanding, ask follow-up questions in an email message.

Also, be sure to thank your interview subject for her time and expertise. This is just good manners, but it is a professionally wise action, too. Your interview subject may one day be a hiring supervisor who reviews your résumé or application for employment.

Finally, compare the results of the interview with other sources of knowledge, for example, other informational interviews, research, and personal experience. Informational interviews are most useful when they are part of a larger career goal exploration effort.

Job Shadowing

Like the informational interview, job shadowing is a great way to learn about your potential career. **Job shadowing** is spending a half-day or whole day following someone at work, so you can see for yourself what the job requires. Like the informational interview, job shadowing requires planning before the experience and some follow up after the experience.

Job shadowing is particularly useful for the following types of college students:

- Students who don't know what to expect from the day-to-day experience of working in their future career field,

- Students who don't already know anyone who works in their career field of interest,

- Students who are undecided or trying to decide between two or more possible careers, and/or

- Students who are unclear about the relationship between their chosen credential and their chosen career.

Use the guidelines below to get the most out of a job shadow experience.

Before the Job Shadow

Come prepared with questions, and prioritize your questions in case you face time constraints. The informational interview questions on page 61 are also appropriate job shadow questions. Likewise, the tips for setting up an informational interview on page 61 apply also to scheduling a job shadowing experience.

During the Job Shadow

Dress appropriately (for example, business attire for an office setting, comfortable shoes for a healthcare setting). You are not going on an interview, so you don't have to wear interview attire. Focus instead on fitting in to whatever setting you will be in. Also, be unobtrusive and observant. Take notes and ask questions when the time is appropriate.

Some challenges in job shadowing include the following:

- It can be hard to find people to job shadow. Start networking now to find someone to job shadow.

- You must rely on the generosity and availability of someone working in your future field.

- Some careers may not accommodate job shadowing. For example, you can't easily sit in on a drug or alcohol counseling session due to privacy concerns.

After the Job Shadow

Write the person that you shadowed a personal thank you note. In your note, include specific details that were useful to you, for example, information your job shadow mentor showed you or told you.

Like with the informational interview, compare the results of the experience with other sources of knowledge, for example, informational interviews, research, and personal experience. Keep in mind that the work environments and cultures vary from company to company.

◨ Conclusion

Now is a good time to reflect on what you have learned from your career goal exploration. Be sure to add any new career options to your record on page 3.

The most thorough career goal exploration combines academic research and personal experience. In order to really know what to expect from a future career, you should compare the facts and figures you learn about from on-line resources with the personal experiences you hear about in informational interviews and with the personal observations you make during a job shadowing experience. Only then can you realistically anticipate what to expect from your future career.

CHAPTER 3
Career Goal Exploration

What is the best source of information to answer the following career goal exploration questions? Consider the specific resources from Chapter 3: the Occupational Outlook Handbook, CFNC, other online resources, the informational interview, and job shadowing.

1. What is the average starting salary?

2. How does a specific company evaluate its employees' performances?

3. What are the credentials required to begin a specific career?

4. What are the credentials required for a specific job at a specific company?

5. What are the daily tasks of a specific career?

6. What opportunities for advancement exist in a specific career?

7. Where in North Carolina and in the United States are the most jobs in the industry located?

Goal Setting

This chapter will introduce you to several resources and concepts to help you begin to set goals based on the thoughtful reflection in the self-assessment stage and the thorough research in the goal exploration stage. Goal setting, like a lot of the concepts in this textbook, is an art and a science. You can learn to improve your goal-setting skills by following the advice on these pages. But until you put the concepts into practice and make the necessary adjustments to make them work for you, you'll just be going through the motions, and you won't see the real benefits of setting and then accomplishing your goals.

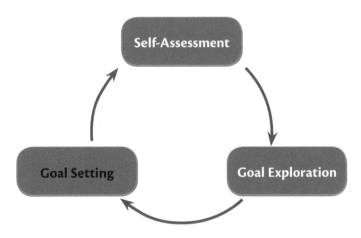

Specifically, Chapter 4 will address the following very useful tools in career goal exploration:

- Strategies for effective goal setting,
- SMART goals,
- Community College Goal Setting Action Plan, and
- Academic Course Plan.

Strategies for Effective Goal Setting

Goal setting is a purposeful way to focus your mind and your energy on what you value most. Goals provide us with a meaningful structure to articulate what we really want for ourselves. Goals also keep us motivated and help us live proactive, not reactive, lives.

Goals can take you from where you are now to where you want to be. You can set goals to improve your study habits, to earn a specific credential, to transfer to a university, and/or to enter a new career field. Use the following strategies to set the most useful goals for yourself:

- **Reflect on the self-assessment stage of goal discernment.** Take into consideration what you learned about yourself from the self-assessments. Write goals that reflect your interests, personality, and values. These goals will be more meaningful to you than a goal that you think you should have for yourself or a goal that someone else sets for you. If you discover that the results of your self-assessments contradict the goals you have previously set for yourself, then think critically about whether you need to revise your goals based on your recent reflections.

- **Incorporate your knowledge from the goal exploration stage of goal discernment.** Use what you learned from your research to make your goals as specific as possible. For example, if you learned that you need a graduate degree to qualify for your chosen career, then write an academic goal that includes the specific required graduate degree. You might also include any preliminary credentials you will earn along the way as objectives that will lead to the larger, long-term goal.

- **Write down your goals.** This is an important step in differentiating between goals and dreams. Consider posting them where you will see them and be reminded of where you are going. You might write your goals on post-it notes and put them by the bathroom mirror or car dashboard to remind yourself what you are working toward.

- **Use "I will..." statements.** When you begin your goal statements with these very important words, you give your goals the power to motivate you.

- **Prioritize your goals.** None of us multitasks as well as we tell ourselves we do. Nor can we concentrate on many goals simultaneously. Organize your goals into short-term goals and long-term goals. Your short-term goals might be related to your academic goals, for example, grades you'll earn this semester or the credential that you'll earn from your community college. Long-term goals, on the other hand, are more likely to be your professional goals, like the career you'll enter when you finish your credential or the path you'll take to advance in your career field. Just make sure that your short-term goals and long-term goals are related, so they'll be meaningful and motivational.

■ **Write performance goals, not outcome goals.** As you think about your academic and professional goals, consider how much control you have. When you set performance goals (instead of outcome goals), you have control over those goals. For example, in preparation for a test, a performance goal would be studying for a specific amount of time or using a specific study strategy. An outcome goal would be to make an A on the test. You might study for a test longer than you've ever studied before and still not make an A because of test anxiety or a distracting testing environment. If you had set an outcome goal of making an A, then this will be a defeat. However, if you set a performance goal of studying for a specific length of time, then you can feel the satisfaction and self-confidence from achieving this goal. And you will be motivated to continue your strong study habits.

■ **Anticipate obstacles.** If you set a goal that you never accomplish, then you should use the experience as an opportunity to learn more about yourself. Did you not reach the goal because it was too big or difficult? Because you were not motivated to do the work that it required? Because you got distracted by a new goal? Whatever the reason, use it to write a better goal the next time. Consider the size and scope of the goal and how easily it fits into the other aspects of your life.

STUDENT NOTES

See page 150 for more information about acronyms.

SMART Goal Setting

As you decide what you want to accomplish academically and professionally, write out your goals and ask yourself if your goals are SMART. Consider the following very common academic goal as you read about **SMART goals**.

"I will make good grades."

Specific	You are more likely to do the work required to achieve a specific goal than a general goal. For example, "I will make good grades" is not specific because different students define good grades differently. Some students consider A's, B's, and C's to be good grades while others consider only A's and B's to be good grades. A more specific goal is "I will make all A's."
Measurable	Establish a way to determine whether or not you achieve your goals. When you can measure your goals, you can figure out how well you are progressing and adapt when necessary. For example, at the end of the semester, you can look at your unofficial transcripts and see if you made all A's or not.
Attainable	Make sure it is possible to achieve the goal. For example, if your goal is to earn all A's, but you are a full-time student and a full-time employee with no time to study for your classes, then your goal may not be attainable. Set yourself up for success rather than failure by writing goals that are possible.
Realistic	More specifically, make sure it is possible for you as an individual to achieve the goal. To reach your goals, you must be *willing* and *able* to do the work that your goals require. For example, if your goal is to earn all A's, and you are willing to put in the work that is required to earn A's, then your goal is realistic. But if you don't prioritize your time to study, then your goal is unrealistic.
Time-Bound	Establish a deadline, so you can know when to evaluate whether or not you have achieved your goal and to create a sense of urgency. Looking back at the poorly written goal, when is the student going to make good grades? This week? This semester? This year?

Look at the following examples to see how to change vague goals into SMART goals.

> **Vague Example 1:**   I will lose weight.
>
> **SMART Revision:**   I will lose 10 pounds in six months by limiting sweets and exercising every week.

This SMART goal is specific and measurable (*lose 10 pounds*), attainable and time-bound (*six months*), and realistic (*limiting sweets and exercising weekly is doable for most people*).

The only SMART criterion that is questionable is whether or not this goal is realistic. If this individual is willing to sacrifice sweets and to add exercise to her weekly routine, then it is a realistic goal.

Vague Example 2: I will pass my classes.

SMART Revision: I will earn a B in BIO 111 and an A in ENG 111 this semester.

This SMART goal is specific and measurable *(naming the exact grades and the exact classes)*, attainable *(students can earn these grades)*, and time-bound *(at the end of the semester, you will find out these grades)*.

The only criterion that is questionable is whether or not the goal is realistic. If this student is willing and able to do the work required to earn these grades, then it is realistic. If the student is unwilling or unable to do the work required, then it is not realistic.

Vague Example 3: I will be successful.

SMART Revision: I will be a self-employed accountant in five years.

This SMART goal is specific *(self-employed accountant)*, attainable *(it is possible to earn an AAS degree in Accounting in less than five years)*, and time-bound *(five years)*.

Again, the only questionable criterion is whether or not the goal is realistic. If this student is willing and able to do the work required to earn the AAS degree and then do the work that is required to become self-employed, then it is realistic. If the student is unwilling or unable to do the work required, then it is not realistic.

Below is a former Durham Tech student's academic SMART goal. Notice that it includes a specific credential that she planned to earn and a timeline.

"In Fall 2016, I will transfer to North Carolina State University and enter the College of Management to earn a Bachelor of Science in Business Management with a concentration in Entrepreneurship. By then I will have an Associate in Arts degree from Durham Tech. In order to be admitted to NC State, I will keep my GPA at 3.0 or higher. I will have to stay in school full time to keep my financial aid, so I'll need to go to Durham Tech for six semesters (counting summer sessions) in order to get my AA degree. I will graduate from North Carolina State University in Spring 2018."

The same student developed an equally strong professional SMART goal. This particular student had developed a business plan in one of her business courses, so her professional goal includes details that many first-semester students are not ready to include just yet. However, most college students can identify for themselves the basic features of a professional goal (for example, the career, the timeline, and the connection between the academic goal and the professional goal).

> "I will open my own pet-sitting small business in 2018. I will continue to work as a part-time pet sitter while I am a Durham Tech and NCSU student to stay connected with the field. I will use the time between graduation and when I open my own business to find investors and execute my business plan. By 2020, I will employ 8 to 10 part-time workers to take care of the company's day-to-day operations."

As you write your own academic and professional SMART goals, use these examples as a guide, and your goals will be just as effective.

● Community College Goal Setting Action Plan

Students in various academic programs can have similar goals. On the following pages are several lists of steps to complete each semester to help you achieve your goals. The chronology of the plan below is a recommendation. You may decide to do some of the activities earlier or later than what is recommended here. You may also find that it will take you longer than four semesters to complete your specific community college program. Add whatever individualized goals you've set for yourself in the margins.

First Semester

- Choose a program and credential that matches your career goals.

- Draft an Academic Course Plan (see page 74), so you can anticipate how long it will take to finish your credential.

- Orient yourself to your community college and start to explore the resources available to you, including career counseling, academic advising, and transfer advising.

- Connect with your academic advisor (see page 207 for tips on working effectively with an academic advisor).

- Create an advising folder and keep all of your important documents in it, for example, your Plan of Study, your Major Pathway or Pre-Major, or Study Track (university transfer students only), your Academic Course Plan, your Registration Forms, and printouts of important messages from your advisor.

- Take your first-semester classes seriously. If your classes are easy for you, then use this semester as an opportunity to develop a strong GPA. If your classes are difficult, then get the help you need to pass them. It is difficult to bring up your GPA after just one bad semester (see pages 190–194 for more information about GPAs).

Second Semester

- Research what additional credentials you will need to succeed in your career.

- Revise your Academic Course Plan (see page 74) based on any new understanding of course availability/scheduling or input from your advisor.

- Look for scholarship information on your community college's websites. Many scholarships require that applicants be enrolled in a specific program.

- Meet with your advisor to select your classes for the next semester and to ask any questions you have about completing your credential.

- Research universities that offer your intended major if you plan to transfer. Watch for university recruiters to visit your community college, and visit university campuses during "open houses."

- Keep a list of classes you have completed or review your unofficial transcript from WebAdvisor.

- Look for extracurricular activities that support your goals.

- Monitor your GPA and notice the impact your grades in a single semester can make on your cumulative GPA.

Third Semester

- Review your Academic Course Plan (see page 74) and make changes as needed. As you finish pre-requisites and enter your program of study, you may find that you have fewer course options each semester. It will become that much more important that you plan a few semesters in advance the further into your Plan of Study you get.

- Update your list of classes you have completed or review your unofficial transcript from WebAdvisor.

- Meet with your advisor to select your classes for the next semester and to ask any questions you have about completing your credential.

Many universities have specific application deadlines. If you plan to transfer to a senior institution, then find out when the university accepts transfer applications. Don't forget to check for financial aid application deadlines, too.

■ Find opportunities to get involved in your future career field. Look for volunteer opportunities, internships, or co-op experiences. You can put your newly developed skills to work while networking with future professional colleagues.

Fourth Semester

■ Meet with your advisor to conduct an unofficial degree audit. Bring your unofficial transcripts and/or your Plan of Study with the classes you have successfully completed checked or highlighted. This will help you identify any classes you still need to take.

■ Meet the graduation application deadline for your community college. Some colleges encourage students to apply for graduation a semester before they plan to complete their program of study. Even if you don't plan to participate in the commencement ceremony, you should apply for graduation. Your application will trigger an official degree audit process that will confirm for you that you have completed all of the required coursework for your credential.

■ If you're an AA or AS student, then schedule an appointment with a transfer admissions counselor or advisor at the university. Bring a list of questions that you have about transfer. Follow up with a thank-you note.

■ If you're an AAS or diploma student, then take advantage of networking opportunities such as job fairs or informational interviews. See a Career Counselor on campus for assistance with creating or updating your résumé and preparing for interviews.

When you finish the Academic Course Plan (see the next section), revisit this timeline and add or move steps to the semester appropriate to your personal timeline.

◯ Academic Course Plan

The **Academic Course Plan** is a chronological and individualized list of the courses you plan to take to earn your specific credential. The Academic Course Plan document is a useful tool to help you synthesize all of the information you learned about yourself, your program, and your future career in the previous stages of goal discernment. Read the example Academic Course Plan that follows and then use the tables on the next pages to plan the sequence of the classes you will take to earn your specific credential. Start with the Plan of Study or Major Pathway/Pre-Major/Study Track that will lead to the credential you will need to accomplish your professional goals.

Hints for Completing the Academic Course Plan

Use your Plan of Study or Major Pathway/Pre-Major/Study Track to complete the Academic Course Plan.

- If you are in a career/technical education or health tech program, then use the Plan of Study.

- If you are a university transfer student, then use your Major Pathway/ Pre-Major/Study Track.

STEP 1: Include any transfer credit or previously completed college credits that will count toward your degree. List these credits in the Semester 1 table at the beginning of the Academic Course Plan.

STEP 2: Include your current schedule for this semester. *[Hint: If you have transfer credits or previous college coursework, then your current semester will be listed in Semester 2 or later. If you have no transfer credits or previous coursework, then you will list your current schedule in Semester 1.]*

STEP 3: When planning your coursework for future semesters, include any developmental education or other pre-requisite coursework that you may need to complete. For example, if you need to take ENG 111, but you placed into DRE 097, then list DRE 097 and DRE 098 in the semesters before you list ENG 111.

Other helpful hints:

- List co-requisites in the same semester. For example, at many community colleges CHM 130 and CHM 130A are co-requisites and must be taken in the same semester.

- Credit hours are the number of hours that will be listed on your transcript and the number of hours that you will pay tuition for.

- Contact hours are the number of hours that you will spend in class, including class, clinical, and lab hours.

Sample Academic Course Plan

This student used the NCSU College of Management Study Track to complete the Academic Course Plan below. The student plans to graduate with the AA degree and then transfer to NCSU to study business. She took the college's placement test which determined that she needed to start with DRE 098. She did not need any developmental math.

Semester 1 (Semester/Year: **Spring 2014**)

Courses	Credit Hours	Contact Hours
DRE 098	3	3.5
ACA 122	1	2

Semester 2 (Semester/Year: **Summer 2014**)

Courses	Credit Hours	Contact Hours
SPA 111	3	3
SPA 181	1	2
BUS 110	3	3

Semester 3 (Semester/Year: **Fall 2014**)

Courses	Credit Hours	Contact Hours
MAT 171	4	5
SPA 112	3	3
SPA 182	1	2
PED 111	1	1
ENG 111	3	3

Semester 4 (Semester/Year: **Spring 2015**)

Courses	Credit Hours	Contact Hours
GEL 111	4	5
MAT 263	4	5
PSY 150	3	3

Semester 5 (Semester/Year: **Summer 2015**)

Courses	Credit Hours	Contact Hours
GEL 113	4	5
ENG 112	3	3

Semester 6 (Semester/Year: **Fall 2015**)

Courses	Credit Hours	Contact Hours
ENG 232	3	3
HIS 122	3	3
ECO 251 (mini 1)	3	3
ECO 252 (mini 2)	3	3

Semester 7 (Semester/Year: **Spring 2016**)

Courses	Credit Hours	Contact Hours
HUM 110	3	3
SOC 210	3	3

STUDENT NOTES

Your Academic Course Plan

Use the tables below to record the classes you have already completed, the classes you are currently enrolled in, and—most importantly—the classes you plan to take in the future.

Your Program of Study: _____

Your Credential: _____

Semester 1 (Semester and Year: _____)

Courses	Credit Hours	Contact Hours

Semester 2 (Semester and Year: _____)

Courses	Credit Hours	Contact Hours

Semester 3 (Semester and Year: _____)

Courses	Credit Hours	Contact Hours

Remember from Chapter 2 that credit hours are the number of hours that will be listed on your transcript and the number of hours that you will pay tuition for. The credit hours are typically listed on all of the college's Plans of Study.

Contact hours are the number of hours that you will spend in class, including class, clinical, and lab hours. You may need to use your college's website to look up the contact hours associated with a specific course.

STUDENT NOTES

Semester 4 (Semester and Year: _____)

Courses	Credit Hours	Contact Hours

Semester 5 (Semester and Year: _____)

Courses	Credit Hours	Contact Hours

Semester 6 (Semester and Year: _____)

Courses	Credit Hours	Contact Hours

Semester 7 (Semester and Year: _____)

Courses	Credit Hours	Contact Hours

Semester 8 (Semester and Year: _____)

Courses	Credit Hours	Contact Hours

Semester 9 (Semester and Year: _____)

Courses	Credit Hours	Contact Hours

Semester 10 (Semester and Year: _____)

Courses	Credit Hours	Contact Hours

⬛ Conclusion

Record your SMART academic and SMART professional goals on the tracking sheet on page 3 for easy reference in the future.

As you set your academic and career goals, keep in mind the important strategies from the beginning of this chapter. Most importantly, remember that the most effective goals are SMART goals. As you prepare to write your SMART goals, you should always consider what you know about your personality, interests, and values from various self-assessments. You should also take into consideration any academic and career research that you have conducted as part of your goal exploration. Goals that are informed by this level of self-assessment and exploration are that much more likely to be achieved. Keep track of your goals and share them with those who will help you achieve them (for example, family, friends, advisors) in order to ensure you stay on course and have the support you need to succeed.

CHAPTER 4
Goal Setting

1. Read the goals listed below and put a check mark under S, M, A, R, and/or T if the goal is Specific, Measurable, Attainable, Realistic, and/or Time-bound. If any of the elements are missing, rewrite the goal to make it SMART. The first one is done for you.

	Goals	S	M	A	R	T
Vague Goal #1	I will improve my time management this semester.			✓	✓	✓
SMART Revision	I will use a weekly planner to keep up with assignments and activities this semester.	✓	✓	✓	✓	✓
Vague Goal #2	I will pass my final exams.					
SMART Revision						
Vague Goal #3	I will graduate with an associate degree in one year.					
SMART Revision						

2. Write one academic goal and one professional goal in the table below. Put a check mark under S, M, A, R, and/or T if the goal is Specific, Measurable, Attainable, Realistic, and/or Time-bound. If any of the elements are missing, rewrite the goal to make it SMART.

	Goals	S	M	A	R	T
Academic Goal						
Professional Goal						

3. Re-read the Community College Goal Setting Action Plan on pages 72–74. Highlight or underline the steps that you will need to complete this semester or next. Also, identify three additional steps that you will need to complete to earn your credential at your community college.

a. _____

b. _____

c. _____

UNIT 2
Learning Strategies

S uccessful students know and apply a variety of learning strategies in college. Depending on your learning style preferences and the subjects you are studying, you may need to use a variety of learning strategies. You may also find that as you progress through your academic program, your classes get more and more challenging, and you need to use strategies that were previously unnecessary. This unit of *Success by Design* will address the following useful learning strategy topics:

Chapter 5   Time Management

Community college students are very busy people. Many students balance academics with work and family. Other students experience more flexibility and unscheduled time than ever before. Therefore, effective time management is critical to success in college.

Chapter 6   Reading Strategies

Reading textbooks and other academic materials takes a very different set of skills than reading a magazine or piece of fiction. Some college students are surprised by the amount of reading that they must complete; this chapter will help you make the most of all of those reading assignments.

Chapter 7   Note-Taking Strategies

Note taking is a critical step in the process of turning new information (through classroom instruction and reading assignments) into the knowledge base that will prepare you for future coursework and your career.

Chapter 8 Study Strategies

Successful college students do more than re-read the textbook and make flash cards to prepare for a test (not that there's anything wrong with flash cards!). This chapter will introduce study skills that will help you maintain your learning in a class as well as prepare for assessments.

Chapter 9 Test-Taking Strategies

Finally, tests give you the opportunity to demonstrate how much you have learned. In addition to fully understanding the course content, it is beneficial to know some techniques that will help you show your instructor the breadth and depth of your understanding.

Important Learning Outcomes for Unit 2

- Demonstrate time-management strategies, including identifying unproductive activities, listing ways to use time more effectively, and showing use of a weekly planner.

- Evaluate learning strategies, including note-taking, test-taking, information processing, time management, and memorization techniques, and identify strategies for improvement.

Unit 2: Learning Strategies Tracking Sheet

As you read Unit 2, record the individual elements of your personal learning strategies in the table below. This will be a helpful record to track your personalized preferences and plans.

Time-Management Goals	Reading Goals
Note-Taking Goals	**Study Strategies Goals**
Test-Taking Goals	**Learning Strategies Strengths**

STUDENT NOTES

Time Management

Oone of the most significant differences between college and high school is the amount of work that college students complete outside of class. Successful college students manage their time effectively in order to take responsibility for their learning in a way that is unlike learning in high school. A full-time course load in college is typically only 12 credit hours because college instructors expect students to spend additional hours each week outside of class reading the textbook, working on assignments, meeting with study groups, and reviewing their notes.

More specifically, college instructors expect students to spend two hours outside of class working on course content for every one credit hour assigned to the course. This is called the **2:1 rule**. For example, if you take a three-credit English class like ENG 111, your instructor most likely expects you are spending six hours per week outside of class learning course concepts or completing assignments. What exactly should you do during these six hours? Most students realize that they should complete assignments. What many struggling students don't understand is that they should also use this time to complete maintenance studying (see pages 142–143 in Chapter 8 for more about the need to study and review notes regularly, not just before an exam) and to complete pieces of larger assignments (for more on breaking up large assignments into manageable tasks, see distributed practice on page 96).

Many students think of time management as a way to manage competing demands on their time. But good time management also allows you to live your values more fully. If you value your family, then you likely spend many hours each week caring for them and doing activities with them and for them. If you value your education, then you will have to manage your time so you can do the necessary activities that lead to your educational goal.

If you follow the 2:1 rule, where will you do most of your learning? On your own or in the classroom? Is this similar or different from the expectation in high school?

Finally, as you'll see later in this chapter, time management is directly related to stress management. One of the first steps that many college students take when they realize that they are experiencing stress is to manage their time more effectively by starting assignments earlier or minimizing time wasters. Indeed, effectively using a planner and using distributed practice will likely become two of the most important tools for achieving your college success goals.

Even if you're already adept at handling a full schedule, college will require you to apply these skills to a diverse range of new tasks. To help you with this transition, there are two tools you should know how to use effectively: to-do lists and weekly planners.

To-Do Lists

A **to-do list** is a list of activities or tasks you need to complete, often during a specific period of time (for example, a day or a week) or for a specific project. Nearly everyone has made a to-do list at some point, but some to-do lists are better than others. Consider these two lists below. Why is Jay's list more effective?

Michael's list	Jay's list
Basketball	1. Look over flash cards for Biology Chapter 3. Quiz tomorrow
Study	2. Call Mom
Clean kitchen	3. Brainstorm thesis and outline for paper due next week
Bank	4. Grocery: milk, bananas, cereal
Email pictures to Sean	5. Call Melanie about party?

One of the greatest values of a to-do list is setting your intentions for the day.

Jay has included two things that Michael hasn't: detail and priority. First, Jay is more specific in his list, and that means his chances of completing his tasks are greater. For example, on Michael's list "study" is so vague that it would be easy for him to skip it. Conversely, imagine you're Jay. Seeing on your to-do list that you need to review your flash cards over Chapter 3 for the quiz tomorrow is so specific that you will likely complete that task. And that's one of the most important things about a to-do list. Sure, it lists tasks for the day, but more importantly, a to-do list sets your intentions. The more specific you are with your intentions through your to-do list, the more apt you are to accomplish them once you've set this goal on paper.

Jay also ordered his list by prioritizing items. It's important to ask yourself three questions in order to rank your tasks:

- What is important?
- What is urgent?
- What is both important and urgent?

Important tasks are those that lead to achieving your goals. Urgent activities usually demand immediate attention, but these are often in response to others' needs or requirements. For example, an important item on your to-do list might be to find out about financial aid for the next semester when the deadline isn't for a few months. If you rely on financial aid to go to college, then understanding your financial aid options is important to your goal of completing your credential. An urgent item on your to-do list might be to ask your instructor about a test that is scheduled for tomorrow.

> Based on the order of his list, what can you assume about Jay's call to Mom?

To effectively prioritize your day's activities, use the following matrix that has been adapted from Stephen Covey's *The 7 Habits of Highly Effective People*. As you can see, you'll complete urgent and important activities first, then items on your to-do list you labeled important but not urgent. Finally, you'll complete urgent items and then those items that are neither urgent nor important.

> Which block of items do you currently prioritize on your list? When should you complete them, according to the chart?

Prioritization Matrix

Urgent, Not Important COMPLETE 3RD	Urgent and Important COMPLETE 1ST
• Interruptions • Emails • Phone calls • Required daily tasks	• Deadlines • Some calls or emails • Commitments, such as meetings, classes, work shifts
Neither Urgent Nor Important COMPLETE LAST	Important, Not Urgent COMPLETE 2ND
• Distractions • Time wasters • Mindless activities, such as watching TV	• Preparation • Planning • Time with friends and family

Urgency (vertical axis) — *Importance* (horizontal axis)

This method ensures that you don't live your life only responding to the most pressing concerns or the ones that evoke the greatest stress. Instead, there's intentionality and design in your day. You control your schedule instead of your schedule controlling you. Strive to spend time on the things that matter most by checking to see that you've been intentional with your day, not just reactive. After you order your list in the method described, see if your to-do list reflects your goals in life.

In addition to the content and order of the list, the method you use for making your to-do list is important as well. Establishing a routine is best. Jotting a note on the back of a receipt is a well-intentioned effort, but not highly effective. Do you really want to take the chance that you'll remember which receipt contains your important tasks for the day and that you'll be able to find it in the bottom of your bag? Many people keep a to-do list in a pocket notebook that they use daily. There are several apps that organize your to-do list, such as Evernote, and many online calendars, such as Google's, through the task list. When they think of something that needs to be done, they get out the notebook and write it on the list. Important reminders and tasks are less likely to be lost using one of these methods. An added benefit is peace of mind, knowing that nothing important will be forgotten.

Also, you should develop a routine for when you'll create and prioritize your list. If you are a morning person, then get up a few minutes early and write out your to-do list before the hectic day begins. If you are a night person, then write your to-do list before you go to bed. If you find yourself having a difficult time falling asleep or feeling anxious at night, writing down your tasks for the next day may provide you relief from stress or anxiety. Many people find that having a place devoted to writing down pending tasks reduces their stress because it starts a plan for completing responsibilities.

In fact, a large component of stress management is effective time management. If you're feeling stressed, your to-do list can help you reduce the feeling of being overwhelmed. Writing things down reduces the mental energy required to keep track of your responsibilities, allows you to prioritize clearly (through the three questions), and also begins the process of accomplishing a goal rather than worrying about a stressor.

◼ Planners

One of the most useful tools to any successful person is a daily, weekly, or monthly planner. A planner is not the same as a to-do list. A planner is much more specific than a to-do list because you select a precise time or date to complete the task on the to-do list. Consider the differences:

To-Do Lists	Planners
Often used for just one day or a specific event	Used continually, usually for a year at a time
Lists events by importance and urgency	Lists events by the date or time of day
Indicates the order in which you plan to accomplish the task; does not indicate at what time	Allows you to set aside a specific date or time to devote to an activity

Many different types of planners are available, but the most important distinction is the length of time you can view across two pages when open. The most common three types are monthly, weekly, and daily planners. Consider the advantages and disadvantages of the examples that follow. Specifically, notice the items listed for the 18th day of the month.

The **monthly planner** allows you to see upcoming events far in advance, which can allow you to see patterns in your activities and keep track of important dates, such as birthdays and due dates.

Sample Monthly Planner

S	M	T	W	Th	F	S
1	2	3	4	5	6	7
			Math study group 11–12			
8	9	10	11	12	13	14
			Math study group 11–12			
15	16	17	18	19	20	21
	Math Test Ch. 6–10		CIS 110 Project 2 due	ENG 111 1st Draft due		
22	23	24	25	26	27	28
		ACA Paper Due	Math study group 11–12		Trey's b'day party	

Notice that important but routine daily tasks are not written on the monthly planner. Now, consider this example of a weekly calendar that follows for the week of the 16th–20th. With a **weekly planner**, not only are planned events noted, but they are also assigned to a specific time for completion. Therefore, while monthly planners allow you to "forecast" your life, weekly planners are more detailed by showing regular events.

Sample Weekly Planner

	Mon.	Tue.	Wed.	Thu.	Fri.
7:00	Drop off kids	Gym	Drop off kids	Drop off kids	Drop off kids
8:00	MAT 121 Test on Chapters 6–10	Gym	MAT 121	Study on campus	MAT 121
9:00	MAT 121 Test on Chapters 6–10	ACA 122	MAT 121	Study on campus	MAT 121
10:00	MAT 121 Test on Chapters 6–10	ACA 122	MAT 121	Study on campus	MAT 121
11:00		ENG 111	Dr. appt.	ENG 111 1st draft due	
12:00	Lunch	ENG 111	Dr. appt.	ENG 111 1st draft due	Lunch
1:00	CIS 110	Lunch	CIS 110— Project 2 due	Lunch	Study on campus
2:00	CIS 110	Work Study Job on Campus	CIS 110— Project 2 due	Work Study Job on Campus	Study on campus
3:00	Study on campus	Work Study Job on Campus	Study on campus	Work Study Job on Campus	Study on campus
4:00	Study on campus	Work Study Job on Campus	Study on campus	Work Study Job on Campus	Study on campus
5:00	Pick up kids	Pick up kids	Pick up kids	Pick up kids	Pick up kids
6:00	Dinner	Dinner	Dinner	Dinner	Dinner

Compare the previous weekly planner example to a daily planner example that follows for Wednesday, the 18th. As you can see, the **daily planner** adds an even greater level of specificity. For this date, the monthly calendar didn't mention any tasks, and the weekly planner only mentioned regularly scheduled activities (plus one due date). The daily planner, however, also includes specific tasks to accomplish instead of the generalities of the weekly calendar. For example, "Make final edits to ENG 111 paper and print" from the daily planner is much more specific than the weekly calendar's "Study on campus." As well, the daily planner notes disruptions to the normal plans, such as the doctor's appointment that's scheduled when the student usually studies on campus and grabs lunch.

Sample Daily Planner

Wednesday the 18th

7 a.m.	Drop off kids
8 a.m.	
9 a.m.	MAT 121 8:00–10:10 Ask about project due next wk.
10 a.m.	
11 a.m.	Doctor's appointment 10:45
12 p.m.	
1 p.m.	CIS 110 1:00–2:20—Project 2 Due
2 p.m.	Make final edits to ENG 111 paper & print
3 p.m.	
4 p.m.	Write interview questions and email contact for ACA portfolio
5 p.m.	Pick up kids
6 p.m.	Dinner—Taco night
7 p.m.	
8 p.m.	Finish one set of math HW problems

As you can probably now see, the monthly planner alone is not specific enough for use by college students. You need a planner that allows you to devote specific tasks to the hours of the day in order to make the most of your time. A weekly or preferably daily planner is necessary for the demands of a college student.

While your planner's display is important, how you use your planner is what matters most. On monthly calendars, write anything that's significant at the date level, such as due dates or birthdays. For a weekly or daily planner, on the other hand, write anything that is significant at the hour level, such as appointments or specific goals for that time, for example, the number of chapters to review or the steps of a project you'll complete. Be as specific as the space allows.

Entry	Example	Monthly	Weekly	Daily
Appointments or one-time events	Study groups or doctor's appointments	✔	✔	✔
Important dates	Due dates or birthdays	✔	✔	✔
Recurring events	Class times		✔	✔
Routine tasks	Lunch or picking up the kids		✔	✔
Specific times for completing items on the to-do list	Completing ACA homework or going to the grocery			✔

In using a planner, skilled time managers will not only include what they need to accomplish and when but also how they plan to accomplish those goals. For example, look at Wednesday, the 18th on the weekly planner. This student plans to spend two hours studying from 3:00 to 5:00 p.m. The student knows what he'll do (study) and when (3:00–5:00), but he doesn't include how. He's left out a level of detail that's crucial to the completion of tasks. Remember, the more specific you are about how you'll use the time, the more likely you are to actually complete the task rather than procrastinate or skip it. Detailed notes in your planner mean you're less likely to choose to hang out with a friend on campus. The likelihood of using time as intended increases with greater specificity listed in the planner.

Luckily, completing this crucial step of planning specific tasks is easier once you have your to-do list in hand. As you now know, a useful planner will have time increments on the side so that you can devote specific tasks to a particular time.

Once you've created your to-do list, you can plot activities in your planner. Remember to consider the rank of importance and urgency you gave a specific task before you settle on a day or time to devote to the task. For example, return to Jay's to-do list at the beginning of the chapter. Jay obviously consulted his monthly planner or flipped ahead in his weekly or daily planner before he wrote his to-do list because he's aware that he has a paper due next week.

Now, it's time for him to plan his day. If this were today's date in his planner, how would you arrange his to-do list by time so he can accomplish the most during his day?

Jay's planner

7 a.m.	
8 a.m.	
9 a.m.	Philosophy Class 9:20–10:40
10 a.m.	
11 a.m.	
12 p.m.	
1 p.m.	
2 p.m.	
3 p.m.	Student Senate meeting
4 p.m.	
5 p.m.	
6 p.m.	
7 p.m.	
8 p.m.	

In order to plan Jay's day, you likely had to ask yourself several questions, including how long each activity would take and when he completed his daily routines (eating, showering, packing lunches for the kids, etc.). To-do lists often don't include routine tasks such as these. Planners often do not either. However, you should consider these things when plotting out the day's events. Compare your completed planner day for Jay with the following example. What did you forget to include? What other considerations might need to be noted when using your planner that to-do lists do not include?

Jay's planner example

7 a.m.	
8 a.m.	
9 a.m.	Philosophy Class 9:20–10:40
10 a.m.	
11 a.m.	Make flash cards for BIO
12 p.m.	Call Mom
1 p.m.	
2 p.m.	
3 p.m.	Student Senate meeting
4 p.m.	Grocery
5 p.m.	Dinner
6 p.m.	Paper: Brainstorm thesis and outline 6:00–8:00 p.m.
7 p.m.	
8 p.m.	

For which class and project did Jay use distributed practice?

Another important aspect of using a planner effectively is dividing large assignments into smaller tasks, which are completed over a span of time rather than all at once. This is a form of **distributed practice.** Distributed practice is the opposite of cramming. It is an effective strategy for time management and for study. See page 141 for an explanation of why cramming doesn't work over the long term in college.

To use distributed practice, find the test date or the due date for a project, paper, or significant assignment and back up two to three weeks. Ask yourself what individual steps you need to complete in order to have the task finished on time. Then, plot these steps on your planner, committing yourself to accomplishing bits of work over a span of time in order to improve your final product and limit your stress. Think of this approach in terms of an eating analogy: it's much easier, healthier, and more enjoyable to eat your meal in bites rather than gulp it down in its entirety in one swallow without chewing! Similarly, you want to allow yourself to "digest" a large project, paper, or assignment. It's unreasonable to expect quality work and learning if you don't allow yourself adequate time to complete the assignment.

Whether your planner has a kitten on the cover or is kept virtually on your iPhone, you must refer to your planner often for it to be useful to you. A planner is only effective if you make use of it. Mark down appointments and events as soon as you hear of them. For classes, this means that you should place test dates and deadlines for papers and projects into your planner as soon as you get the course syllabus. You can evaluate how well you're using your planner by completing the Time Management Self-Evaluation at the end of this chapter.

Procrastination

Procrastination is waiting until the last minute to begin a project. Nearly all of us have procrastinated on an academic assignment or project. While you may have had some short-term success with procrastination, you also caused yourself unnecessary stress, did not submit your best effort, and failed to acquire the skills or knowledge the instructor intended the assignment to develop. You also set yourself up for some self-defeating assumptions; ask people why they procrastinate, and most will tell you it's because of a character flaw, such as laziness. In reality, the problem is poor planning and the inability to identify the true difficulty.

If you find yourself putting off tasks, you need to determine the reason you're procrastinating. Students procrastinate because they're overwhelmed by the size of the assignment, unclear about the expectations, unsure how to begin, or uninterested in the work. To determine why you're waiting until the last minute, ask yourself what you're avoiding by waiting to begin. Often, procrastination is merely a means of avoiding something we'd rather not deal with. To overcome your procrastination, ask yourself "What am I avoiding?" Realizing the answer to this question can actually empower you to complete the task.

Often the answer reveals something you didn't realize was affecting your behavior or coursework. With this realization, you may find it easier to begin tackling your task. For example, are you avoiding starting your English paper because you don't know how to research the topic? Realizing this problem will allow you to find reasonable and achievable solutions, such as working with a reference librarian, talking to classmates for tips, or making an appointment to see your instructor during office hours.

The answer to the question "What am I avoiding?" will help you find the real reason you're not tackling your responsibilities as planned. Once you have the answer to this question, try these methods to help you start your project.

Strategies for Overcoming Procrastination

■ Ask yourself what advice you'd give to a classmate or friend facing the same problem. Sometimes you're too close to the situation to see clear solutions. If you think about the reason you're avoiding the work from a more neutral perspective—such as a friend's or classmate's point of view—you may be more likely to think of several reasonable solutions.

■ Set up rewards for yourself. Find an incentive that motivates you, and then determine what work you need to accomplish in order to receive your reward. Tell yourself that if you complete your outline, you'll treat yourself to a coffee, watch a half hour of TV, or look at your favorite website for 15 minutes. But you need to be firm about when you'll use these entertaining distractions, or you'll continually find yourself losing valuable time you need for something else. Grant yourself a precise amount of time to enjoy something fun and then get back to work.

■ Divide the task into smaller pieces so it won't seem as overwhelming. For example, divide writing a paper into six parts: brainstorming, researching, planning, drafting, revising, and editing. Each individual part is completely manageable. The enormity of the task may be intimidating and preventing you from starting. See page 142 for more information on distributed practice.

■ Remind yourself of the task's purpose. Ask yourself what you can get out of the assignment, so you don't see the project as an exercise you *have* to complete but as an opportunity. Reading and taking notes on two Anatomy and Physiology chapters not only will fulfill your homework assignment, but it will also make you more knowledgeable once you're a health care professional. You might not be interested in becoming a computer engineer, but learning how to create an Excel spreadsheet in your class could help you make a budget or add another skill to your résumé.

- Just do it. It's been said that the hardest part of running for most people is just getting off the couch and putting on running shoes. Similarly, starting the assignment for a student is often the hardest part. At some point, you just have to make yourself open the book and begin.

Conclusion

Mastering effective time management is one of the greatest challenges in college. With the transition from high school to college, responsibility for learning largely shifts from the teacher to the student. Understandably, students struggle to adapt to new expectations—such as the 2:1 rule and more complicated schedules—while also trying to overcome ineffective past behaviors, such as procrastination.

However, with practice, the tools outlined in this chapter will help you make better use of your time. Utilizing distributed practice, prioritizing to-do lists, assigning tasks to specific times in your daily planner, and using the strategies for overcoming procrastination will all be worth the effort when you find balance for your competing priorities, experience less stress, learn more, and achieve better grades.

Record your goals for improving your time management habits on the tracking sheet on page 85 for easy reference in the future.

Time Management Troubleshooting

Problem	Solution
Waiting until the last minute to start papers or projects	• Ask yourself, "What am I avoiding?" • Use distributed practice by placing due dates in your planner as soon as you get your syllabus, backing up several weeks, dividing the paper or project into smaller steps, and then plotting those individual tasks in your planner.
Starting your homework 10 minutes before class	• Use a planner. Write assignments down after every class and then check your planner several times a day to make sure you're on track to complete everything. Adjust if you are not. • Do first the homework you least want to work on. • Realize your motivation for completing the class or college.
Feeling like there isn't enough time in the day	• Use a planner to devote a specific time to accomplishing your daily activities. • Prioritize by asking yourself what is urgent, what is important, and what is both urgent and important. Complete the tasks according to level of urgency and importance.
Wasting time	• Remind yourself of your goals for college or the course. • Use a planner to stay focused by plotting your daily to-do list and routinely checking your planner throughout the day to make sure you're on track to accomplish your goals. • Use fun activities as a reward for completing less-desirable tasks. Set limits for these reward activities and stick to them. If you finish your paper, play basketball for 30 minutes and leave when that time is up. • Complete the Time Management Self-Evaluation at the end of this chapter. Revise your schedule and activities if your priorities and actual activities don't align.
Not following your planner	• Keep your planner in a way that makes sense to you. If you're obsessed with your smartphone, keep your planner on it. • Create a to-do list and then plot it in your planner. Be specific in your entries. • Consider if your planner meets your needs. Are you using a monthly or weekly planner? Switch to a daily planner. • Complete the Time Management Self-Evaluation. Revise your schedule and activities if your priorities and actual activities don't align.
Not knowing where all your time goes	• Complete the Time Management Self-Evaluation. Revise your schedule and activities if your priorities and actual activities don't align.

CHAPTER 5

Time Management

1. Using the three questions to prioritize your to-do list, rank this student's to-do list. In the left column, write I for important and U for urgent. Remember, some items may be both urgent and important, so label them with both letters. Some items may be neither, so don't label them. Then, on the right, rank the items in the order the student should complete them, with 1 being the first task to complete.

Urgent? Important?	Task	Priority
	Read psychology homework (due in two days; won't be graded)	
	Study for math quiz (in four days; 2% of total math grade)	
	Interview for ACA portfolio (due in four weeks; 25% of total ACA grade)	
	Research financial aid options for next semester	
	Look at brother's vacation photos online	
	Return library books (due yesterday)	
	Go to the tutoring center for help with English paper (due in one week; 20% of total English grade)	

2. Create a to-do list of the things you need to accomplish this week. Then prioritize these tasks by asking yourself the three prioritization questions and using the matrix.

3. In your own words, what is distributed practice?

4.   Select a big project or paper you have due for a class. Apply the strategy of distributed practice by dividing this project into smaller individual tasks. List each step.

5.   What are the differences between a planner and a to-do list?

6.   What are the three planner types? Which planner type is best for you? Why?

7.   What should you ask yourself when you realize you're procrastinating?

8.   What are your two biggest time wasters? How will you manage them? Write two goals to help you overcome these time wasters.

9. Tina has a serious problem with procrastination. She wants to be a successful student, but she gets distracted easily and lacks the discipline to make herself use distributed practice to study. She is taking ENG 111 for the third time, and she has to pass the course this semester because the college's policies state that a student cannot enroll in the same course more than three times without special permission. She failed the course the first two times because she always read the assignments and wrote papers at the last minute. What strategies can you recommend that Tina use to stop procrastinating?

10. George has a 20-page research paper for his Abnormal Psychology class due at the end of the semester. The instructor asked that an annotated bibliography, an outline, and a rough draft be turned in at the same time as the final draft. George is feeling overwhelmed because he is taking three other courses and has many assignments to complete for the other courses as well. Help him map out a plan of action for his Abnormal Psychology research paper, so he can fulfill the requirements without minimal stress.

Time Management Self-Evaluation

Even the most self-aware planners can find themselves having difficulty meeting all their obligations. These moments often occur when we face a new challenge. Times of transition, such as starting a new job, beginning college, or switching semesters can throw the best of planners off course. When your time management needs an adjustment, a time management self-evaluation can help.

The two tables on the following pages can help you identify your problem. Complete **Log 1: Planned Week** according to the instructions below. After finishing Log 1, turn your attention to **Log 2: Actual Week**, so you can see how well your actions matched your intentions. Then you can begin to problem solve to learn how you can use your time effectively.

Log 1: Plan Your Next Week

1. In the blue row at the top, write the days of the week, beginning with today. For example, if today is Wednesday, write W, TH, F, S, S, M, T across the top row.

2. Write down your specific commitments. Class, work, meditation or religious activities, and family or social events should be marked down. Also mark out the hours you sleep, which should be no less than eight hours per day. You may want to color-code your schedule with highlighters.

3. Now, with your weekly to-do list in hand, write in the specific times when you'll accomplish your tasks. Don't forget to consider time you'll need to commute, prepare meals, shower, clean, work out, and complete other important routine tasks.

4. Be sure to include some personal downtime, which is necessary for physical and psychological health.

5. Next, devote specific time to study. Consider the time of day you learn best. Also, make sure you set aside enough time to learn. Remember the 2:1 rule as you schedule your study time. If you are taking 12 credit hours, then you should be studying 24 hours per week.

Is all of your time every day already allocated after step 2 of Log 1? If so, you need to reconsider your schedule because you're overcommitted. While you may think you're maximizing on the little time you have, by depleting this resource you're not allowing yourself to be successful. The unexpected will happen, and you'll need time to deal with unplanned events, such as transportation problems or illness. You should not expect yourself to calmly and responsibly address unplanned events if you do not provide yourself the time to do so.

Log 2: Record Your Actual Week

1. Label the top row in the same way as Log 1.

2. Throughout the next week, account for all of your time by recording your activities in the second table at the end of each day.

3. Evaluate your results with the questions that follow the logs.

Log 1: Planned Week

6 a.m.							
6:30							
7:00							
7:30							
8:00							
8:30							
9:00							
9:30							
10:00							
10:30							
11:00							
11:30							
noon							
12:30							
1:00							
1:30							
2:00							
2:30							
3:00							
3:30							
4:00							
4:30							
5:00							
5:30							
6:00							
6:30							
7:00							
7:30							
8:00							
8:30							
9:00							
9:30							
10:00							
10:30							
11:00							
11:30							

Log 2: Actual Week

6 a.m.							
6:30							
7:00							
7:30							
8:00							
8:30							
9:00							
9:30							
10:00							
10:30							
11:00							
11:30							
noon							
12:30							
1:00							
1:30							
2:00							
2:30							
3:00							
3:30							
4:00							
4:30							
5:00							
5:30							
6:00							
6:30							
7:00							
7:30							
8:00							
8:30							
9:00							
9:30							
10:00							
10:30							
11:00							
11:30							

Self-Evaluation

At the end of the week, analyze your use of time by answering the following questions:

1. What surprised you most about your use of time?

2. For what tasks did you not budget enough time?

3. What activities were most difficult to complete as intended? Why?

4. What time wasters prohibited you from staying on track?

5. What activities did you procrastinate starting? Why did you avoid completing them?

Your honest answers to these questions can help you more effectively use your time and accomplish all of your weekly responsibilities. Don't get discouraged if your two logs look dramatically different. Keep in mind that building good time-management habits takes time.

If you are a time-management novice, begin improving your use of time by selecting the strategies that will be most useful to you. What one or two strategies would yield the greatest results? Focus on improving in these selected areas rather than incorporating every strategy in this chapter.

If you are more experienced at managing your time, identify the two or three areas you could improve. What could help you do better? How are you not using your time to your advantage? Now is a good time to build strong time-management habits in preparation for more demanding classes—and schedules—in the future.

Reading Strategies

Instructors often assign college students to read textbook chapters, articles, and online content. However, students sometimes fail to understand what an instructor means by "reading" an assignment. Moving your eyes from left to right down the page is not what instructors intend for you to do. When an instructor assigns reading, he or she actually means any number of the following activities:

■ Learn the material on the assigned pages and be ready for a quiz.

■ Make note of material on the assigned pages you don't understand and ask questions.

■ Begin some foundation work on this concept, so you will be prepared for lecture or in-depth analysis of the concept in class.

■ Comprehend what's on these pages and be prepared to contribute to class discussion on this topic in the next class.

■ Know this material for an upcoming class activity.

While instructors' intentions for your reading may vary, what doesn't change is an instructor's expectation that you not only read the material, but that you understand it as well. Some material is easy to comprehend. However, since college introduces you to many new ideas, how do you understand what you've read when topics are complex, foreign, or even uninteresting to you? The answer is actually very simple: Be active—not passive—when reading.

Many students *think* they're being active readers by using a highlighter or pen to underline important ideas. However, highlighting and underlining are actually passive techniques. Think about it: a six year old can be given a highlighter and manage to mark bold terms and numerous sentences in a college textbook. Does this mean that she understands what she has read?

STUDENT NOTES

Absolutely not! Highlighting and underlining are passive reading techniques because they do not require you to do anything with the concepts; you're simply marking up your book. All you have to do to highlight or underline is move your marker or pen across the page in a somewhat straight line. How does that make you think? How does that help you process or understand information? While you may have used highlighting and underlining with some success previously, as you move into higher-level college classes the material will increase in difficulty, and you'll need different skills to make sense of the material.

For this increased difficulty, you'll need to use active reading strategies. **Active reading** forces you to interact with the presented ideas through annotating, or taking notes while you read. During active reading, you write notes in your book or on a piece of paper. While you may already make a few notes here or there—such as when you encounter a new term—active reading is more than this. Active reading requires you to ask questions, compare new information with your past knowledge and experiences, note your reactions and judgments to what you've read, and consolidate ideas in brief summaries. There are many active reading methods you can research and use, but all of them have the following basic components, which can be remembered through the acronym **PSAR: Prepare, Survey, Annotate, Review**.

> What do you do when you read? Compare your usual methods to the PSAR strategy presented on the next few pages.

◻ Prepare

Prepare Yourself

Before you read, make sure you're ready to learn and have set realistic expectations. At the end of a day, your body and mind don't have the necessary energy to tackle learning new material. Additionally, we often learn material in small chunks rather than in lengthy quantities. Nevertheless, many students wait until the end of the day to read dozens of pages. Be more reasonable by dividing your assignment into smaller sections to read at more optimal times of the day. For example, if you need to read two chapters for Thursday, read five pages at a time over four to five days by using your breaks between classes and time during lunch.

Set an intention. Be specific about how much you want to read in a certain amount of time. For example, if you have an hour between classes, it would be realistic to read and take notes on 15 pages. If you reach your goal, reward yourself. You could go for a walk later, meet a friend in the cafeteria for lunch, watch your favorite TV show that night, or call a friend after class. These rewards provide a much-needed mental break to refresh your concentration and motivation. Reward yourself when you reach your goals, but also make sure you get back on track so you don't find yourself getting drawn into watching more TV than you intended or not finishing the rest of your reading.

Also, estimate your reading time effectively. College students often underestimate the amount of time actually required to read and understand a text. On average, students read about 200 words per minute when learning. College textbooks contain about 350–400 words per page; therefore, you can probably read about one page per two minutes. However, this estimate does not include time to make notes (see the A of PSAR) or time required to make sense of particularly dense material. Therefore, it's much more helpful to estimate between three and four minutes per page of reading. Use this guide to help you plan your time effectively. If you have a reading assignment that contains twenty pages, you'll need between an hour and an hour and twenty minutes to understand the material and complete your reading. Consider how much you need to read and provide yourself adequate time to complete the reading to ensure better comprehension.

> The estimate that you'll need three to four minutes per page of text is a generalization. What factors affect whether you can read the material at a faster pace? What factors would force you to slow down?

This estimate also does not consider your familiarity with the material. If you are reviewing a topic you're familiar with, it's a good idea to **skim**. When you skim a textbook chapter, you usually read the following parts:

- the first paragraph of the chapter,
- the first two lines and last line of the other paragraphs, and
- the last paragraph of the chapter.

If you see any unknown terms, names, or dates, if there are illustrations or charts that don't immediately make sense, or if you are confused, you should stop skimming and instead read that information carefully. After you skim, you should be able to state the main idea and provide a general overview of the text. If you cannot, you should go back and make sure you have read the first and last paragraphs and the first two lines and last line of all other paragraphs. If you still cannot summarize and state the main idea, you need to go back and read more. You weren't as familiar with the topic as you thought.

Finally, prepare yourself for reading by taking care of your body. Eat small, healthy meals throughout the day and make sure you're getting enough rest. Studying after a large fast-food meal isn't very productive. Also, avoid caffeinated or sugary drinks; although they may provide a quick energy boost, these short-lived periods of energy are followed by an energy slump. Prepare your body and mind to be alert.

Prepare Your Environment

> What are your biggest distractions when reading? What do you need to do in order to minimize those distractions?

Create a space that's conducive to learning new material. Let your friends and family know that you're studying and can't be reached. Turn off your phone and put it out of sight. Go to the library or find a room with a door you can close. Avoid common areas where you might run into people you know or overhear conversations.

STUDENT NOTES

 ## Survey

After you've prepared yourself, **survey** the text. Start by looking at the table of contents in the beginning of the book to see what you'll be learning and how it fits with other course information. Within the assigned chapter or section, look for chapter headings and subheadings and turn these into questions. Think about what you already know about the material. Begin finding connections between the material and your personal life or previous academic experience. For example, if you looked at the table of contents for Chapter 9 of this book, you'd see the following list. Look at the comments to see how you could achieve some of the mentioned goals of scanning this chapter:

By surveying the text in this way, you'll have an easier time staying focused because you'll be more invested in discovering answers to your questions and seeing if your ideas are mentioned. You can also scan the chapter for bold or italicized words to see how much new vocabulary you'll be learning. Unlike skimming, which aims to improve your overall understanding of a chapter's main topic, **scanning** usually has the goal of locating specific information within the chapter. When scanning, you usually have a specific target in mind, such as finding bolded or italicized words. Scanning is particularly helpful during the R step of PSAR, reviewing. See the Review step for more on scanning.

Annotate

To actively read, you must have a pen or pencil in hand and you must annotate. **Annotating** is taking notes while you read. It's easiest to make notes in the textbook, but you can also annotate in a notebook.

For examples of methods you can use when taking notes in a notebook, see Chapter 7.

Why annotate? Because students' biggest problem with reading isn't that they can't comprehend the material, it's that they don't think enough about the content. Annotating forces students to interact with the material, which helps make sense of the ideas presented and allows readers to recall the information later. Annotating also makes reading less painful because it provides a specific task to accomplish when reading: compiling a list of important notes. In other words, annotating is a simple process that makes it easier to understand what you read.

What kinds of things should be noted? How is annotating actually done? Consider this guide:

Note	Specifically	How to Annotate
Important Information	Definitions, terms, significant examples, helpful diagrams	Develop a consistent system. For example, box key terms, star significant examples, and circle helpful diagrams.
Questions	Questions you have as you read	If your question isn't answered by the time you finish the assigned material, ask your instructor in class.
Responses	Your reactions to the material	How do you feel about what's being discussed and the way the author presents it? Draw a smiley face if the concept is funny or seems like a great idea. If the topic seems confusing, draw a frowny face with a question mark above it.
Conclusions	Brief summaries	Write a few words or sentences per section to summarize the main ideas. You'll process the information and create a reference for when you need to study for the test.

One of the reasons this book has wide margins is to provide the space for you to annotate the material. Try annotating page 161 from Chapter 9 on test-taking strategies in your book. Then, look at the annotating example on the next page to compare your annotations with the ones completed here.

Annotating Example of Page 161 in Chapter 9:

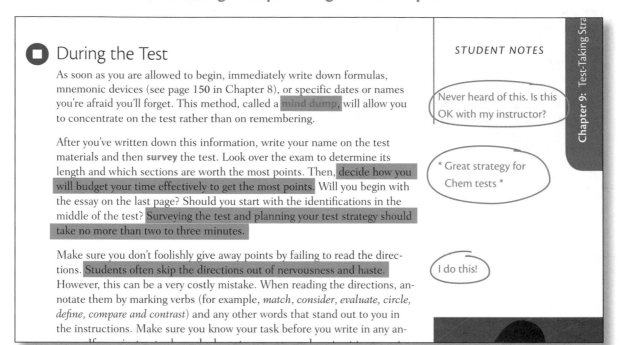

Examine the annotations this student made. Of the four things to note when annotating (important information, questions, responses, and conclusions), which did this student include? Did she forget any?

Review

After you read, **review** the material. Scan your textbook and notes for terms, examples, or ideas presented during class lecture. Remember, when you scan, you have a specific target in mind. Since you probably read the material before class lecture, it would be a good idea to scan your book for terms the instructor introduced, especially if you still have questions about a concept. Annotate these ideas if you did not previously. You may not have realized how important these ideas were when you first read the chapter. It's a good idea to revisit the chapter, scan for particular topics, and then re-read sections to answer questions you may still have after the instructor covers the material.

Look over your annotations periodically to keep the information fresh. Taking five to ten minutes to review notes while they're fresh helps commit them to memory. You will fill in gaps more easily than if you wait until before the test to review your notes. This short review can save you tons of time later when you're studying for a test or completing a project. In this way, your annotations are great reference tools, since they likely include the most important information from the chapter. Reviewing these annotations is more time-saving than re-skimming or re-reading the entire chapter.

You can also try reciting your notes. Shut your book and put away your notes. Speak aloud what you've learned. You can divide this up by heading or section. Check back in your book. What did you have a hard time explaining? What did you not remember? Make note of that information in your annotations. Reciting notes can be especially helpful to verbal learners (see Chapter 1 for descriptions of specific learning style preferences).

Don't forget that reviewing your notes can also help you get more out of your time in class. Review annotations and other notes right before class to prepare for the day's lessons, discussions, and activities.

Using PSAR Strategically to Overcome Common Reading Problems

When reading, students often have problems in one of two areas. Either they cannot remember specific points and facts they've read (supporting details), or they cannot recall overarching concepts (main ideas). Some of the problem may lie in students' learning style preferences. For example, sensing learners may more naturally focus on definitions and specific facts while ignoring abstractions or large concepts. On the other hand, intuitive learners may be drawn to large themes and relationships between ideas when they read, not paying as much attention to details. See Chapter 1 for more information on learning style preferences, including tips for developing a more balanced approach to acquiring new knowledge. When encountering such problems while reading, return to PSAR and use the mnemonic to improve your reading strategy. Here are two ways to tailor PSAR for common reading problems.

> Mnemonic devices are memory tools. Learn more about them on page 150 in Chapter 8.

Difficulty Remembering Large Concepts after You Read

Prepare: Set your intentions on seeing the larger picture of what you read. Tell yourself that while you will not ignore details, you will not concentrate on them alone. Write the questions "How?" and "Why?" at the top of your notes, so you'll concentrate on these while reading and not the "What?," "Where?," "Who?," and "When?"—usually items of detail.

Survey: Look over the chapter and turn the headings and subheadings into questions. Examine questions at the end of the chapters, especially those that ask about relationships between ideas, such as essay questions. Keep all of these questions in mind as you read the chapter.

Annotate: As you read, summarize sections or paragraphs. Periodically return to your list of questions (from Survey step) to see if you're able to answer any part of them. Continually try to answer the questions "How?" and "Why?" as you read.

Review: After you've read, try to answer the questions you've posed. Recite your answers aloud to make sure you really can explain what you've learned from the readings. If you cannot, return to the text and re-read. Keep in mind that introductions and conclusions often contextualize, connect, and summarize main ideas and key concepts.

Difficulty Remembering Specific Information after You Read

See pages 143–144 in Chapter 8 for tips on using flash cards effectively.

Prepare: Set out flash cards to write down specific information. Also have various highlighters on hand to categorize information: blue as definitions, yellow as important names, and pink as other specific information of note.

Survey: Look at how the author notes specific information. Are terms or names bolded? Are key terms listed at the beginning or end of the chapter? Write these items on the front of flash cards.

Annotate: As you read, write on the flash cards any other specific items you read. Highlight the information in the text according to the color key you determined earlier.

Review: Test your knowledge in two ways. First, look at each flash card you created during the survey step and try to write your understanding of that term's significance on its backside. Double-check your answers with the information in the chapter or in the glossary if your book has one. Also, look at the headings and sub-headings for each section. Can you provide the answer aloud for each of these questions in each section: who, what, when, where, why, and how? If so, you have a great understanding of what you read. If not, go back and find the answers in the chapter.

Conclusion

Remember that reading requires adaptation. You'll read a wide variety of texts in college, and you shouldn't assume that just because you're a skilled reader in one subject that you'll be as proficient a reader in another area. Reading material varies, as does what your instructor or discipline expects you to take away from the reading. While you may read and understand specific and detailed information well—such as definitions and formulas in a math or science class—you may have a harder time in classes that focus on broader themes—such as theories in a philosophy class or cultural developments in a history class. When you find yourself struggling in a class, examine your reading style and adapt your focus within PSAR to those areas of greatest importance to the course.

Keep in mind, too, that reading is a skill that requires practice, and everyone can improve his or her reading. While completing the steps of PSAR may seem time-consuming, the more you practice them, the more ingrained they will become and the less effort you'll need to use them. You'll not only become faster, but you'll also understand more of what you read.

STUDENT NOTES

Record your goals for improving your reading strategies on the tracking sheet on page 85 for easy reference in the future.

Reading Troubleshooting

Problem	Solution
Struggling to understand what you read because you encounter words you don't know	• Use the context surrounding the word to try to determine its meaning. • Divide the word into its parts (affixes) and use these to help you narrow the definition. • If you still don't know the word, look it up in the book's glossary or in a dictionary. If you don't have a dictionary with you, use an online resource, such as www.dictionary.com. • Keep a log of new words and their meanings in the back of your notebook. Review these periodically.
Getting bored or distracted	• Revisit the P of PSAR. See page 111 for tips on adequately preparing your environment. • Remember that reading doesn't just require your eyes. To read actively, you must have a pen in your hand, and you must be taking notes. • Make sure you're annotating well. Don't just mark new words, dates, and names. Challenge yourself to write a question, response, and/or conclusion for each paragraph. • Revisit the S of PSAR. Survey the chapter to ask questions. Turning chapter headings into questions will help you concentrate and read with the intent of finding their answers. Having a question in mind can invest you more in reading to find the answers.
Having trouble remembering what you've read	• Focus on improving the A of PSAR. Annotating requires you to interact with the text, which is key to remembering the information. How could you annotate better? • Turn chapter headings into questions and quiz yourself by trying to answer the questions verbally. • Be strategic in your PSAR approach. See the two approaches on pages 115–116.

CHAPTER 6
Reading Strategies

1. Without looking back in the book, can you name the steps of PSAR? Can you explain aloud to yourself the meaning and importance of each step? If you've forgotten any of them, return to the chapter, scan for PSAR, and then reread that section.

2. What should you do before you read? Why?

3. Use the steps below to practice the S step of PSAR and survey Unit 3 of this book.

    a. Turn the title, headings, and subheadings into questions.

    b. What connections can you make between the material in Unit 3 and what you've already learned in this class?

    c. What connections can you make between the material in Unit 3 and your personal life?

    d   What connections can you make between the material in Unit 3 and your previous academic experiences?

4. Of the S and A steps of PSAR, which do you think you're most likely to forget to do? How will you make sure you do it?

5. Do you usually complete the R steps to reading? If not, how will using these suggestions pay off?

6. Examine your current use of annotating. Look at any two pages in Chapter 2, which you've already read. Use this checklist below to assess your annotating skills.

Annotating checklist

☐ The page is marked with multiple symbols and drawings so that I can locate important information quickly.

☐ I've written questions in the margin.

☐ I've written responses in the margin.

☐ I've written conclusions in the margin.

If you have not placed a check in any of these boxes, go back and review the information for that concept on pages 112–113.

7. Keisha is in her first semester of college and is taking 10 credit hours: ACA 122, CIS 110, PSY 150, and developmental math. She never tried very hard in high school but still managed to graduate with a 3.0 GPA. She's doing well in her classes, except for CIS 110 and PSY 150. Both regularly have multiple-chapter reading assignments. In PSY 150, she's failed her first test and all three of her quizzes. In CIS 110, she hasn't had a test yet, but she feels completely lost. She's frustrated with the classes. She blames her instructors for not teaching well and is thinking about dropping the classes. Based on this chapter, what advice would you give to Keisha to help her with her problems?

8. Natasha is almost ready to transfer to a four-year institution to pursue a degree in English. She's taking the last of her courses, including BIO 112 and HIS 131. Unfortunately, she's not doing well in either class. She finds that she can't remember the specific terms the instructors test over. She does well on the essays and short-answer questions, but she fails the matching and fill-in-the-blank sections. She's embarrassed because she's done the reading assignments but still can't recall what she's read. Plus, she's even questioning her ability to pursue an English major because she is doubting that she can read and understand different texts. What two strategies from this chapter do you think would help Natasha most?

Note-Taking Strategies

I n college, it is assumed you're taking notes over readings and activities during class because writing things down helps you remember them, especially if you're a visual learner. College tests cover much more material (often three or more chapters) than exams in high school (often only one chapter or section). You cannot expect yourself to remember information from a class lecture that took place a month ago if you only listened. Another reason notes are so important in college: they are great reference tools. You can go back and review the recorded information from your notes, but if you just listen in class, you have nothing to refer to. Also, your notes will often contain information that will be necessary to know for a test, presentation, paper, or project. Finally, taking notes keeps you active during the class. You'll be more focused and engaged and less prone to distractions and a loss of concentration. Research shows that the better your notes, the better you do in the course. Taking notes is a surefire way to indicate to yourself that you want to pass a course.

> Annotating, or taking notes while you read, is discussed specifically in Chapter 6.

● When to Take Notes

While there are times you should be taking notes outside of class, most students think they know when to take notes during class: when the instructor writes on the board. However, passively copying only what the instructor writes on the board onto paper is not effective. Taking notes requires active thinking and listening. Besides, there are many other times throughout class when you should be writing down important information. Here are some additional times you should be taking notes.

Class Discussions

Note instructors' questions as they lead class discussions. Your classmates' responses and instructors' comments on those responses should also be written down. They'll likely appear on a quiz or test or will be expected to be addressed in an assigned essay.

Student-Led Presentations

Instructors try various methods to present information to students. Sometimes they assign students to present the information to each other in order for students to practice communication skills and to meet learning goals for the course. Often during peer presentations, other students do not take notes because the information is not directly coming from the instructor. However, think like the instructor. Why is he devoting valuable class time to student presentations? What does he want you to learn from the activity? Consider these questions and use the answers to guide your note taking during peer-led presentations. Add to your notes anything the instructor asks the group or adds to their presentation.

Group or Paired Activities

As with student-led presentations, many students erroneously assume that group work or activities aren't note-worthy. If an instructor spends valuable class time to work in pairs or groups, you should include the information or experiences from these efforts in your notes. Don't just take notes to report back. Take notes as the activity is discussed or analyzed, too.

Explanations of Assignments

Often, you're presented with an assignment sheet for important projects or papers. While the instructor discusses the assignment, make notes in the margins of the assignment sheet, so you'll have additional guidance when you begin work. When discussing an assignment, instructors often provide important tips and explanations based on past students' performances, and this advice will be very helpful to you as you complete yours.

Demonstrations

Don't forget to have your notebook and pen ready for important information the instructor points out during demonstrations. Just because you're huddled around a lab table, car engine, or practice "dummy" doesn't mean you shouldn't bring along your note-taking supplies to write down questions, explanations, or tips.

◉ What to Take Notes On

Always begin your notes by writing down the date, class, and topic. By writing these things down, you'll know when notes were presented. If your instructor puts an agenda on the board for each class, make sure you copy it down at the beginning of your notes for the day. Having the agenda within your class notes will be like having a table of contents for that day's notes. Also, you'll process the expectations of the class and be more focused on the class's progression by knowing what to anticipate next.

Most importantly, during class write down any information that **SOARS** above the rest. That's anything that is

> **S**ingled out,
> **O**n the board,
> **A**sked,
> **R**epeated, or
> **S**tressed.

Singled Out

Your instructor will spend time addressing significant terms, processes, dates, events, or examples, which should signal to you that this information is important. When the instructor singles out information by devoting time to it as a topic, you should write it down. Conversely, when he or she mentions a word, name, or date in passing, that's usually the instructor's way of providing extra information, not core class content, so that information isn't always necessary to write down. However, if time is spent singling out an idea for discussion or elaboration, then it is note-worthy.

> Information that's singled out often can be put on flash cards, so when you review your notes after class, go ahead and make your flash cards. See pages 143–144 for tips on making and using flash cards.

On the Board

This category not only includes board work, but also information projected from the computer or overhead. When the instructor spends time and/or energy presenting terms, diagrams, outlines, or other information on the board or overhead, you should write this information in your notes. Try to use the same formatting as your instructor since it may be a form of a visual organizer that can help you understand relationships between concepts. (For additional tips about taking notes over PowerPoints, see page 134.)

Asked

Write down questions posed by the instructor, those asked by classmates, and any questions that pop into your head while listening. Write down the answers as well. Make sure to follow up on any unanswered questions after class. Often, the questions posed by the instructor appear on future quizzes and tests.

Repeated

Any terms or explanations repeated by the instructor should be noted. Listen for main ideas that are revisited as well. If time is spent reviewing a concept in class, this should signal its importance. Make note of what the instructor says about it.

Stressed

Instructors rarely literally say "This is important!" Instead, it's expected that you infer the significance through verbal and non-verbal cues. When the instructor pauses, changes her tone of voice, or varies her pace of words, she may be implying that the information is crucial. Also, watch for gestures she makes with her hands or arms, as well as any underlining or circling of items on the board. Make a note of the information the instructor is stressing and why.

Think like the instructor to write better notes. Instructors are charged with covering a large quantity of content in little time, so they must be efficient and clear. Consider how your instructor accomplishes this. What does she spend time and energy on? Making a handout? Creating a presentation? Defining important terms in class? Demonstrating a process? Get in the mind of your instructor by considering why she is presenting the information to realize what is most important and what should be included in notes.

How to Take Notes

Do you find yourself writing down too much information? Do you not refer back to notes you've taken? If so, the problem may be that you're not taking notes effectively. Follow these recommendations to make your notes more helpful.

Before Class

Separate your class notes either by committing one notebook for each class or by using a large binder and keeping notes for each class under separate tabs.

Prepare yourself mentally by ridding your mind of any outside thoughts or distractions. When you walk through the classroom door, tell yourself that you're leaving your emotional stressors outside the door until class is over so that you can concentrate.

Be physically prepared, as well. Get enough sleep the night before. Use the bathroom, have a small snack, or get a drink before class begins, so you won't be distracted. Eating during class means you're not concentrating fully on taking notes.

It's a good idea to review your notes from the previous class and annotations you took while reading your textbook. If you've marked questions from homework, reading, or review, read over them so you'll know what you need to ask your instructor to clarify.

Upon arriving to class, sit where you won't be distracted. Don't sit in lab near the guy who spends class time on Facebook. The temptation to watch what he is doing—rather than keep up with the instructor and your notes—will be too great. You need to not just hear, but to listen and think about presented material in order to take good notes. Make sure you have all your necessary supplies. Get them out before class begins and start writing down the class, date, topic, and agenda.

During Class

To take good notes, you need to avoid distractions. Put your phone on silent and place it in your bag. Only keep on your desk what you need for taking notes. To stay focused, notice when your mind wanders and come back to the activity by writing down the topic the instructor is discussing at that point. Put a question mark in the margin where you drifted so that you can fill in your notes later.

STUDENT NOTES

While taking notes, it is important not only to consider what SOARS but also the layout of your notes. Make sure you don't cover your entire notebook paper with writing. Instead, leave white space on your paper. About two inches of white space on the side or bottom of your notes will allow enough room for you to add additional information and questions when you review your notes. You can also put question marks in the unused white space when you don't understand something, so you will remember to ask the instructor after class. As you take notes on the presented material, don't forget to write down your own reactions or thoughts that arise as you listen. Were you surprised? Was something odd or funny? Did something remind you of a concept from another class or your real-world experience?

It's nearly impossible to write down everything that's said in a class period. It's also entirely ineffective. Writing down only the information that SOARS above the rest will allow you to capture just the important information, but you might still need to be faster in your note taking. Therefore, don't write concepts down word for word. Use short phrases instead of full sentences and paraphrase or summarize information.

Abbreviating common words or phrases also helps capture more information rapidly. You can use common abbreviations or you can try omitting all the vowels of longer words to speed your note taking. Incorporating new abbreviations into your note taking will take some practice, but they soon become ingrained. Most importantly, devise a method that you will understand and use, so that you can move from focusing on how to take notes (method) to the ideas presented (content). See the following table for some common abbreviations.

> Mark the abbreviations you don't use but could begin using this semester.

Abbreviation	Longhand
ppl	people
info	information
gov't	government
natl	national
diff	different
thru	through
b/c	because
b/w	between
b4	before
w/	with
w/o	without
imp	important

Abbreviation	Longhand
aka	also known as, name changed
ex	example
@	at
+ or &	and
–	decrease or less
+	increase or more
=	equals, is, means
→	results in, leads to, caused
vs	against, as opposed to
♀	woman
♂	man
∆	change, transform

In addition to regularly using abbreviations and developing your own shorthand, there are several note-taking methods that you can use to help organize your notes. The informal outline, two column, and Cornell methods model well-tested patterns for note taking. In the following examples, the students are taking notes on the same class lecture in a biology class. Compare the format and content of these notes to see if you can determine the characteristics of each style. Don't worry: you don't need to know anything about biology to be able to evaluate the notes.

Informal Outline

This **informal outline** method visually organizes the presented material by spacing information out on the page. Don't underestimate the importance of visually organized notes, especially if you have a visual or kinesthetic learning style preference (see Chapter 1 for information about learning styles). You can "see" relationships between items and infer them without thinking about them once you've taken notes in this form.

There are two advantages to notes taken in informal outline style. First, the method allows you to show relationships between ideas without spelling them out. How? Items of greater detail are placed underneath their larger group terms. Have a look at the note-taking example on the next page. You can tell that 1, 2, and 3 are all cell theories because they are all listed under the "CELL THEORY" heading. Also, the more to the right the item begins, the greater the level of specificity. While "TYPES OF CELLS" is a general term that lacks additional or detailed information, we can know that cells are divided by their functions, two of which are synthesis and reproduction, levels of details that are far from the left margin due to their level of specificity.

Further, items of similar importance are spaced at the same distance from the left margin. "Membranes" and "Organelles" are equidistant from the left margin. That equal positioning indicates that they are also of the same relative importance. In comparison, the fact that membranes function like a wall with holes in it is a detail that's not as important as knowing what organelles are and their basic functioning. Informal outlines convey these relationships succinctly without spelling them out in words.

The second characteristic of this note-taking method is the use of white space at the bottom of the page. Notes should be reviewed as soon as possible after class, and not more than 24 hours after the class ends. When reviewing notes, you need space to write down summaries, questions, and additional information you may have missed during class. You must leave space to allow for such reviews. Therefore, do not cover the entire page with information. As you take notes, leave the bottom third to quarter of the page blank for later comments and questions. Leaving space for review is critical, which is why all three methods discussed in this chapter require leaving white space.

Later in this chapter, you'll find strategies for what to do when reviewing your notes.

Of course, the challenge of this note-taking method is writing in outline form, especially for an instructor who does not present the information in such a linear, clear format. However, the more you practice this format, the easier it will become.

Informal Outline Example

	4/18 Lecture: Cells
	TYPES OF CELLS
	Many different kinds of cells
	Ex: single, multiple, animal, plant
	Diff. defined by cell structure and function
	Ex: reproduce, synthesize
	CELL THEORY
	1. All living things made up of cells
	2. Cell=basic building block of life
	3. Cells come from other cells that already exist
	CELL PARTS
	1. Membranes
	No matter what kind, all cells have membrane
	Barrier btwn cell + outside enviro
	Like a wall w/holes select molecules can pass thru
	2. Organelles
	????
	* KNOW STRUCTURE—links on Sakai to online videos; will be on test
	* Cells come from pre-existing cells—Where did THOSE original cells
	* come from?*
	* Ask inst. about organelles b/c I don't understand

Two Column

Another note-taking method is the **two column** design. Here, you fold the paper in half, making a crease down the center of the paper. You take notes only on the right side of the crease. When you review your notes, write a question on the blank left side that corresponds to the ideas on the right. In effect, you've created a self-test (page 145 in Chapter 8). You can easily quiz yourself by folding back the answers. Review the questions and when you need to check your responses, unfold the flap.

Two Column Example

	4/18 Lecture: Cells	
○	*What are 4 types of cells?*	TYPES OF CELLS
		Many different kinds of cells
		Ex: single, multiple, animal, plant
		Diff. defined by cell structure +
		function
		Ex: reproduce, synthesis
	What are the 3 cell theories?	CELL THEORY
		1. All living things made up of cells
		2. Cell=basic build. block of life
		3. Cells come from other cells that
		already exist
	What are the cell parts?	CELL PARTS
○		Membranes
		No matter what kind, all cells have
		membrane
		Barrier btwn cell + outside
		Like wall w/holes select molecules
		can pass thru
	What are organelles?	Organelles — ????

Cornell Method

Unlike the informal outline method, the Cornell method of note taking does not use hanging indents or specific spacing to indicate relationships between concepts. However, the **Cornell method** does create sections designed for specific types of notes and reflection, as do the other two methods. The Cornell method of note taking, also called the **T method**, requires you to divide your note-taking paper into sections before you begin taking notes. To do this, draw a vertical line about two to three inches from the left-hand margin. Draw a horizontal line about three inches from the bottom of the page. Your paper should look something like the example below.

Cornell Method Example

	Questions	Notes
	4/18 Lecture: Cells	
	What are 4 types of cells?	TYPES OF CELLS
		Many different kinds of cells
		Ex: single, multiple, animal, plant
		Diff. defined by cell structure + function
		Ex: reproduce, synthesis
	What are the 3 cell theories?	CELL THEORY
		1. All living things made up of cells
		2. Cell=basic build. block of life
		3. Cells come from other cells that already exist
	What are the cell parts?	CELL PARTS
		Membranes
		No matter what kind, all cells have membrane
		Barrier btwn cell + outside
		Like wall w/holes select molecules can pass thru
	What are organelles?	Organelles — ????

Summaries	
	* KNOW STRUCTURE—links on Sakai to online videos; will be on test
	* Cells come from pre-existing cells—Where did THOSE original cells come from?
	* Ask inst. about organelles b/c I don't understand

Begin by writing your in-class notes into the larger right section (labeled "Notes" in the example). During and after class, write in the left quadrant any questions you have as you take notes or as you review them, such as ideas you don't understand, questions posed by the instructor, and possible test questions. At the bottom, write summaries of the information as you review it. The notes contain the same information as the informal outline method and the two column notes, so you can easily compare and contrast the three note-taking methods.

STUDENT NOTES

How do the questions asked in the Cornell method vary from those asked when using the two column method?

After Class

Don't just shove your notes in your bag at the end of class and forget about them. Before you rush out of the classroom door, consider doing the following:

- Look over your notes to see if you need to clarify any of your abbreviations or ask any questions. Fill in gaps or talk to your instructor before you pack up and leave.

- Write down the "muddiest point"—something you still don't understand and need clarification on. Try to find clarification in your book or notes. If you can't, ask your instructor.

- Write a one-minute summary. Spend just a minute writing down what you learned from the class.

Never allow a classmate to borrow your notebook! Go with the classmate to a photocopy machine while he makes copies. Your notes are too valuable to risk losing.

After class, review notes immediately—and definitely within 24 hours—to commit the information to memory. Why should you look at your notes so soon after you've taken your notes? The information is still fresh in your mind but not exactly "learned" yet, so you have the opportunity to solidify that knowledge before you forget it by reviewing your notes within 24 hours. However, if you wait until before the test to study—which can be several days or weeks—those ideas will only be a fuzzy memory and will take much more work to learn.

Many students don't review their notes because they don't know how. Staring at what you've written isn't a good way to learn the information. Try these ideas, which appeal to several different learning style preferences.

- Color-code your notes by starring, highlighting, or underlining items of similar importance. For example, you may put dates in blue, processes in yellow, and key terms in a box. Items that might be on the test could get a star.

- Try to identify four to five main points. Do this in the white space you left on the pages of your notes.

- Share or compare notes with a classmate.

- Try to come up with two or three points or questions for class discussion.
- Follow up with the instructor if you have questions.
- Recite your notes or quiz yourself out loud.

A Few Tips on Taking Notes When They Are Provided

I should be taking notes on notes? Really?

Yes, really! It will allow you to process the information better.

Instructors sometimes provide students with copies of lecture notes, PowerPoint slides, or other material that's discussed in class. Some students make the mistake of equating these photocopies to their own set of notes. If you just rely on what's already copied for you, you're not gaining all of the benefits of active note taking, such as processing the information or remembering what you've written. Having a written record of class information is just one benefit of note taking.

If your instructor gives you the notes before class, write down explanations and points not written on the handouts. Try to identify the main points. Since the basic information is already written down for you, focus on understanding the relationships between the presented material and analyzing it. Also, focus on thinking critically. Ask, "How? Why? So what?" since the "Who?" and the "What?" are likely provided in the notes. Then, review these notes after class just as you would your own.

Conclusion

Record your goals for improving your note-taking strategies on the tracking sheet on page 85 for easy reference in the future.

Learning to take good notes requires practice before it becomes habitual. Remember, the point of taking notes is not only to have an accurate record of information presented in class. The acts of selecting what information to include, deciding on a format, and actually writing the ideas on paper are important steps in learning the material and committing it to memory.

To improve upon your current method, think of note taking as a three-step process: preparing to take notes, writing down what SOARS in one of the three note-taking formats, and then reviewing your notes after class. Just as mastering note taking itself requires some practice, so too does learning how to make the most of the notes you've taken. All too often students stuff their notes in their bags at the end of class, forgetting about them until it's time to add more information during the next class. However, reviewing your notes by writing questions, summaries, and comments in leftover white space within 24 hours of the class meeting is a critical step of the process. Begin practicing better note taking now so that you'll have mastered a successful and reliable method by the time you enter higher-level, more difficult courses.

Note-Taking Troubleshooting

Problem	Solution
Not knowing what to write down	• Review SOARS.
Writing longhand (in complete sentences)	• Use abbreviations. • Summarize ideas. • Paraphrase ideas.
Covering the entire page with writing	• Leave a blank space at the bottom or side of your notes for questions when you review your notes. • Skip lines. • Review the note-taking methods, such as informal outline, two column, and Cornell methods.
Not being able to keep up with the instructor	• Put a star in your notes when you get behind and move on with the instructor. After class, either get notes from a classmate or ask the instructor what you did not write down about that concept. • Use abbreviations. • Practice taking notes in outline form.
Doodling in the margins or losing concentration	• Ask yourself why this material is important. If you don't know, ask your instructor (in a polite and sincere tone, of course) why this material is important or how it fits into other concepts you've studied.

STUDENT NOTES

CHAPTER 7
Note-Taking Strategies

1. What are three reasons you should take notes?

2. Review the list of activities during which you should take notes (pages 123–124). During which of these activities do you usually fail to take notes?

3. What does SOARS mean? When should you use it?

4. What abbreviations—other than those listed on page 128—do you use? Swap lists with a classmate or two to add some new abbreviations to your note taking.

5. How soon after class should you review your notes?

6. Read these notes with abbreviations. What do they mean?

Mesopotamia

today aka: Syria, Iran, Iraq, Turkey

past aka: Babylonia, Sumer, Akkadia

Assyria

many Δs in rulers

wanted b/c of location

  1. Tigris + Euphrates rivers imp. for trade

  2. fertile soil

Δ ⟶ wars over religion + laws

7. After examining the three methods of note taking—the informal outline, two column, and Cornell methods—name the advantages and disadvantages of each method. Is one method better suited to certain types of content? What do the methods have in common? Which do you prefer? Why?

8. Evaluate Jose's notes below. What three pieces of advice would you give him to improve his notes?

⬤	Wrist and Forearm Rotation
	Page 324
	Rotating is moving back and forth from supination and pronation
	Pronator Quadratus
	Pronator Teres
	Supinator
⬤	See Sakai

Study Strategies

S tudy is the first thing many students cut from their schedules because there's not an immediate repercussion for dropping it—no zero on an assignment, no public embarrassment from classmates, no disappointed looks from instructors. But dropping studying will affect you greatly in the long run, both in terms of your grades and in terms of your stress.

Besides making the time to study, another difficulty students encounter with studying is knowing how to study. You know you're supposed to study, but what are you supposed to do, exactly? Unfortunately, many of us were never taught helpful study methods. Instead, many of us just open the book and stare at the pages, hoping that somehow the information will just magically make sense to us and that we'll be able to remember it. Instead of hoping for a miracle, try some of the specific and proven study methods in this chapter when it's time to study.

Many college students also don't know when to study. Novice students will often wait until the last minute to study. This is called **cramming**, and while you may have had some short-term success with this method (in fact, you may have been able to pass a test or two), you won't be able to continue using this method. As you advance in your studies, the material and concepts you're expected to master will become more difficult, and cramming just doesn't work for a large volume of complex material. Secondly, college courses build upon concepts from previous courses, and you're expected to have understood and retained information from previous classes. Cramming doesn't allow for long-term recall. Finally, your future employers will expect you to remember information from your college courses. For example, do you really think your employer—or patient—will forgive you for forgetting important parts of the anatomy when you're a nurse?

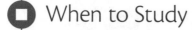

When to Study

So when should a student begin studying? Think about dividing your purposes for studying into two categories: **maintenance**, which allows you to keep up with important information from class to class, and **preparation**, which is studying that prepares you for a specific task, such as a test, midterm, final, oral exam, or project.

Maintenance studying is the reviewing and reading you complete after each class to learn new material. Continual studying that allows you to learn new material must become habitual. Too many students skip this kind of studying altogether. One of the easiest ways to maximize what you discussed in class is to review your notes as soon as possible, and definitely within 24 hours of the class session. We don't naturally remember new ideas the first time we hear them, but if an idea is repeated or reinforced soon after it's introduced, the information will be solidified in our memory. You'll be amazed at how this simple technique can help you process ideas and remember them.

> Review notes within 24 hours of taking them.

When most students think of studying, they envision **preparation studying**, which is targeted study that readies you for a specific application of your knowledge. Many students, unfortunately, wait until the last minute to begin this kind of studying. However, which of these sounds less stressful? Studying 20 minutes a day for eight days or studying six hours in one night? Luckily for us, the less stressful method is also the more effective method. Studying for shorter intervals (for example, 20 minutes) over a longer period of time (for example, eight days) is called **distributed practice**, and you should use this when preparing for tests. In your planner, you should have written the date of the test when you received your syllabus. Back up two to three weeks before that date, and write down when you'll study, the duration (for how long), and the specific method you'll use so that studying becomes a part of your to-do list for that day.

> For more information about distributed practice and using your planner, see Chapter 5.

During both maintenance and preparation phases of study, you must eliminate distractions and create a work environment. On campus, go to the library and find a secluded spot. Sitting at a table in the middle of the library likely means you'll hear a lot of noise and may be interrupted by friends and classmates. Instead of sitting in plain view, find a spot downstairs out of view so that you'll be more likely to study uninterrupted. At home, set up a quiet spot away from family and the TV. Turn off your cell phone. Close the door if you can. Let others know that you need to be left alone for an hour. Sit at a desk or table. Lying on the bed or resting on the couch indicates relaxation and isn't a good way to signal to yourself or others that you're actively engaging in learning.

You should also have realistic expectations about learning the material. While some classes may seem easier than others, you will definitely encounter difficult classes in college. Don't set your expectations for college based on your easiest classes. Instead, expect that you'll need to do whatever it takes to learn. This means that you'll likely need to reread material, find and use resources (for example, instructors' office hours, tutoring, study groups, examples on the Internet), employ multiple study strategies, and struggle. Expect that you'll need to invest many hours and much energy to master material rather than assume you'll comprehend everything the first time you encounter it.

One final note about studying: remember that the first time you do something, it takes more effort than it will in the future, and you will not likely maximize on the results the first time you try it. Keep refining your study methods, stick to the guidelines discussed above, and have patience as you find study strategies that work best for you.

How to Study

As mentioned earlier, most students don't know what they should actually do when they're studying. Listed here are some specific study methods with explanations and examples. Don't try to do all of these methods at once. Select the methods that best match the course material or your learning style preferences (see Chapter 1 for more information about learning styles).

Color-Code Your Notes

Develop a system in which different colors correspond to different types of notes, and when reviewing your day's notes, color-code the information. For example, you can highlight all definitions yellow, use pink to indicate an important example, and mark in blue important questions your instructor posed and then answered. You'll process your notes while "coloring" and in the meantime will make your notes easy to review later. This technique may be especially well-suited for students with visual or kinesthetic learning style preferences.

Make Flash Cards

Flash cards are helpful in two situations: when you have a large volume of very specific information to review, such as multiple definitions of key terms, numerous dates, or important vocabulary (see "Mitosis" example on the next page); and when there are multiple pieces of information to remember for a single concept or idea, such as the steps to investigate a leak in a line or the three most common comma splice errors (see "Bay of Pigs" example on the next page).

To use flash cards effectively, place the concept or word you need to know on one side, and the important information to remember on the other side. Use a rubber band or card case to carry your cards with you, so you can flip through them while waiting for the bus or when you have extra time between classes. This technique can be helpful for all types of learners and can be adapted. For example, you can draw on the cards instead of (or in addition to) writing the words if you find that helps you remember information.

You may also want to write the chapter number the material or terms came from in the corner of the card. This can help you easily determine which of your flash cards you need to study when it's time to review for a test over a specific chapter.

Flash Card Examples

front

Mitosis

back

Ch.2

process in which a single cell divides to produce 2 identical daughter cells

front

Outcome of Bay of Pigs Invasion

back

– Deaths of Cuban & Am. soldiers

– Tarnished Kennedy's presidency

– CIA officials forced to resign

– Castro gained Cubans' support

– Castro turned to U.S.S.R. out of fear of future U.S. attack—beg. of Cold War

Create Self-Tests

You often know what material will be on a test before your instructor hands it to you, so why not create your own version of the test as practice beforehand? There are several ways you can come up with the questions. You can use the questions the instructor posed in class. The questions at the beginning or end of the sections, chapters, or units in your textbook are also usually important. As well, you can turn the review at the end of chapters into questions, turn section headings from the book into questions, or use questions you had while taking or reviewing your notes. Make sure you can answer these questions by jotting down a response and then looking up the information to check, correct, or refine your answer.

You and a classmate could also create two different self-tests and give them to each other; each partner could check the other's answers. If you create the self-test early enough, you can ask your instructor to help you with the questions you did not understand. You can also search for practice tests online. A sample self-test for CIS 110 is below.

Self-Test Example

Chapter 1: Intro to Computers Self-Test

_____ 1. Hardware   a. programs that tell the computer what to do

_____ 2. Software   b. permanent memory

_____ 3. RAM   c. working memory

_____ 4. CPU   d. the "worker"—carries out the instructions

_____ 5. ROM   e. the interface that boots up your computer

_____ 6. BIOS   f. the physical components of a computer

7. What are the differences between input and output devices?

8. What part of the computer is considered the "brain" and why?

Complete the Practice in the Book

In classes such as chemistry, math, and foreign languages, the textbook likely contains practice or problem sets. Although you may complete some of these as assignments from the instructor, you could also complete those not assigned if the material has been covered in the class. Some books even have answers to these questions in the back. When completing the practice, make sure that you don't just do the first ones, as the level of difficulty often increases with the question number. Try a selection of the easy, medium, and difficult questions and then check your answers. Ask your instructor if you have questions.

Review Graded Homework, Tests, Projects, or Papers

If you missed points on an assignment, it most likely means you didn't understand a concept. It also means you'll likely miss similar questions in the future if you don't spend time analyzing your mistakes and learning from them. Spend time with your instructors' feedback and ask questions if you don't understand.

Form a Study Group

For many people, studying in a group is an effective way to learn material because group members can pool their collective knowledge and also benefit from others' perspectives. Similarly, many learning style preferences are served by the interactivity of study groups, specifically active learners and verbal learners. However, keep in mind that students only reap the benefits from study groups when expectations have been clearly communicated. Follow these guidelines to ensure the effectiveness of your study group:

- Set up a specific time and location to meet that is free from distractions. Make sure you include both a start time and end time so that the conversation stays on topic. Keep in mind that it's better to meet multiple times for shorter periods rather than for one long session.

- Assign specific content to every member so that each person has a responsibility. This not only keeps each participant active in the group, but also is a time-saving way to cover a lot of material. This method, called a **jigsaw**, requires each member to be responsible for teaching a specific chapter or concept to the rest of the group. Once each person contributes his "piece," the entire puzzle (for example, test or chapter) has been reviewed by the group.

- Clearly indicate what's expected of each participant. Will she provide a handout? Go over specific examples or problems? How long should each part take?

- Select members for the study group by evaluating classmates' dependability, attitude, communication skills, and study behaviors. You don't want to ask someone to be in a study group if he doesn't turn in his work, arrives late, seems unapproachable, or doesn't take notes.

- Keep the group small—between three and five members. Make sure everyone shares email addresses and phone numbers with all the other members of the group.

- Remember that you don't have to meet in person every time. Email practice questions to each other or exchange lists of important terms to work on before you meet in person.

Create a Visual Organizer

Arranging information into charts or diagrams gives you something to do while studying, and in the process, you come to understand, assimilate, and therefore learn the material. Here are three well-known visual organizers and examples of each.

Venn diagrams are useful to compare and contrast two to three items. For example, if you are asked to write an essay on the similarities and differences of two civil rights leaders, a Venn diagram would be a great place to start.

Venn Diagram Example

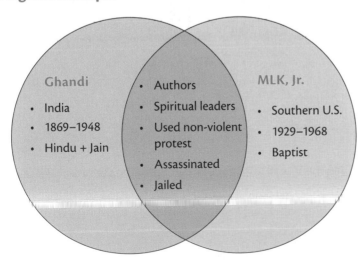

Notice that there are two circles that overlap. In the non-overlapping part of the left circle, all the information pertains only to Ghandi. Similarly, in the non-overlapping part of the right circle, information only pertaining to Martin Luther King, Jr. is written. You can see that Ghandi lived from 1869–1948 while Martin Luther King, Jr. lived only in the twentieth century. Items in the non-overlapping areas indicate how the two civil rights leaders contrast. Similarities are written in the overlapping parts of the circles. Both Ghandi and Martin Luther King, Jr. were authors and used non-violent protest, for example. Venn diagrams allow for a visual representation of similarities and differences. Placing information into a Venn diagram while studying is a great way to prepare for essay test questions.

The **informal outline** is another visual organizer that allows you to visualize quickly the detail and importance of items. Creating an informal outline serves three purposes. First, important terms and people are identified. You should be able to define them all. Second, the informal outline succinctly sums up the most important ideas of the chapter or topic. It's a summary and you should know each part. Finally, it's an excellent visual representation of relationships between ideas. The more to the left an item is placed on the paper, the more general the concept. Items further to the right are more specific and give details and examples. In the following example, there are two modern philosophies and characteristics of each. If you find a concept further to the right, such as "tabula rasa," the term represents a more specific idea.

Informal Outline Example

```
Modern philosophy
    Rationalism
            Knowledge comes from logic/reason
            Ancient Greeks
                Socrates
            Mathematicians of 1600s
                Descartes
                Spinoza
    Empiricism
            Knowledge comes from experience
            Ancient Greeks
                Aristotle
            Philosophers of 1600s
                Sir Francis Bacon
                John Locke
                    Tabula Rasa
```

The order in which items appear emphasizes relationships between concepts. If items appear equally spaced from the left margin, they have the same level of importance (such as Rationalism and Empiricism in the previous example). Information that appears underneath an item but further to the right (such as Socrates) explains, provides details, or gives an example of the concept above it. While many of us learned formal outlines at some point, informal outlines are often just as helpful when studying, so don't worry if you've forgotten the order of numerals and letters that formal outlines require.

Based on this example, you can infer a wealth of information. Take Descartes and Spinoza, for example. With minimal writing, you can see that Descartes and Spinoza are mathematicians of the 1600s who follow the philosophy of rationalism, which holds that knowledge comes from logic and reason, not from experience. You can also see that they are not Ancient Greeks or empiricists.

Like Venn diagrams, you can also find commonalities between ideas. For example, since empiricism and rationalism are the same distance from the left margin and both are under the heading "Modern philosophy," you can infer from the outline that both empiricism and rationalism are modern philosophies.

Much like outlines, **concept maps** are helpful when there's a lot of material of varying importance or specificity to process. A concept map allows you to see connections between ideas. Begin with the most central idea and place it in a circle in the middle of your page. Next, place related ideas, such as examples or divisions, in circles and connect them to the main idea with lines. Keep creating circles, labeling them with definitions, examples, or divisions, and connecting them to larger ideas with lines. It's a good idea to make concept maps in pencil as you will likely need to erase because you're processing the information as you decide which circles to connect and at what level to include information. You might also experiment with Smart Art features in Microsoft Word to generate a concept map.

Much like the informal outline, the concept map allows for a very quick visual reference. By tracing lines to their connections, you can infer a lot of relationships and facts. For example, when you look closely at the following concept map, you see that John Locke and Sir Francis Bacon both connect to "Philosophers of 1600s." You can conclude that both Locke and Bacon are not only philosophers who lived during the seventeenth century, but also by tracing the line connecting "Philosophers of 1600s," you can conclude they are also empiricists and not rationalists or followers of Eastern philosophy.

With all visual organizers, the important thing to remember is that creating these is the learning process. When completed, you'll have a great visual reference, but it's the act of making one—deciding what goes where—that allows an exercise through which you can assimilate, comprehend, and remember information.

Concept Map Example

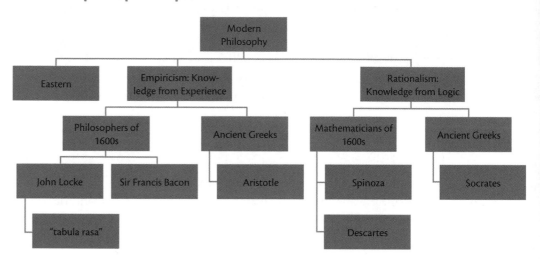

Use a Mnemonic Device

Mnemonic devices are memory tools that allow you to recall a large amount of specific information by creating a memorable word, sentence, or rhyme. Have you ever had to memorize the steps to a process or important details but found that it was difficult to remember everything? Generally, our brains cannot remember more than five to seven items at a time. Also, recalling the order of items is often difficult when the sequence matters. Organizing large amounts of information into a memorable word or sentence allows us to remember more details and their arrangement. In fact, acronyms, acrostic sentences, and rhymes can help you remember that information for a test and even for years after.

One of the most common types of mnemonic devices is the acronym. An **acronym** is a word that helps you remember information and the order of items. In an acronym, each letter represents a different word or set of words. You probably have used these before to remember information. Do you remember PEMDAS or FANBOYS?

Parenthesis	**F**or
Exponents	**A**nd
Multiplication	**N**or
Division	**B**ut
Addition	**O**r
Subtraction	**Y**et
	So

Thousands, perhaps millions, of students have learned the order of operations and coordinating conjunctions using these acronyms, and many can still recall the correct steps to solving mathematical equations and can connect independent clauses years later because they learned these acronyms.

Sometimes, the information you need to learn doesn't form a clear word. In that case, a different mnemonic device—an acrostic sentence—might be more useful. An **acrostic sentence** allows you to remember the order of steps or events as well. You actually probably already know a few. Does this sound familiar: My Very Elegant Mother Just Sat Upon Nine Porcupines? Or, My Very Eager Mother Just Served Us Nine Pies? Many students learned the order of the planets, starting with the one closest to the sun, through one of these sentences. The sentence is interesting enough to recall, and students can remember all the planet names in the correct order by using the first letter of each word. This acrostic sentence is much easier to remember than an ordered list of planet names.

My	Mercury
Very	Venus
Elegant	Earth
Mother	Mars
Just	Jupiter
Sat	Saturn
Upon	Uranus
Nine	Neptune
Porcupines	Pluto

How do you remember the number of days in a month? You might recite the well-known verse below:

Thirty days hath September,
April, June, and November;
All the rest have thirty-one
Excepting February alone:
Which has twenty-eight, that's fine,
Till leap year gives it twenty-nine.

STUDENT NOTES

Many of us use this **rhyme** and others to remember very detailed information, such as the last dates of the 12 months. You can create your own rhymes for information you're struggling to commit to memory. The rhythmic, repetitive sounds will help recall the next line of information.

Often, you don't have to invent your own acronym, acrostic sentence, or rhyme. Google your topic and the word "acronym," "acrostic," "rhyme," or "mnemonic" to see if you can find some existing helpful mnemonic devices. There are also YouTube videos of performed songs or rhymes on numerous topics that you can view to help you remember a long list of items.

Create a Cheat Sheet

Create a **cheat sheet** for every test, exam, or quiz. Of course, do not actually use it unless your instructor allows you to do so. The act of making the cheat sheet will cause you to recognize which information you haven't mastered and then consolidate and review important information. In fact, once you make your cheat sheet, you often wouldn't even need it if you could use the cheat sheet. To create your own cheat sheet, divide an index card into sections by drawing lines. Organize information into these sections in a way that makes sense. Perhaps formulas go in one section, important definitions you have trouble remembering in another, and steps to an important process in the last. Organizing the information in these ways equates to making a type of visual organizer and will help you remember the information.

Cheat Sheet Example

Formulas:

Standard Form	Slope Intercept Form	Slope
$ax + by = c$	$y = mx + b$	$\dfrac{y_2 - y_1}{x_2 - x_1}$
$-a/b = $ slope	$m = $ slope	
$c/b = y$ intercept	$b = y$ intercept	
$c/a = x$ intercept		

Tricky:

• slope of perpendicular line = negative reciprocal

• slope of parallel line = same

Negative slope	Positive slope	Zero slope

Visualize

Like visual organizers, the practice of visualizing concepts appeals to many of us because most of us have a visual learning style preference. Seeing the material, especially in motion, will allow you to absorb the information and remember it better.

Try to imagine the process in your head. In your mind's eye, can you see the process or ideas being described in the reading or notes? You don't have to rely only on your own imagination. You can Google the term and review the results under "Images" and "Video," or you can search for the term on YouTube or well-respected, free sites such as Khan Academy. There are many interactive sites with demonstrations, models, and graphics that bring to life the information discussed in your textbook or class lecture. For example, gear ratios can make a lot more sense if you see the concept explained as someone takes apart a transmission and points out the gear teeth rather than if you just read the definition in your book.

Use KWL

KWL is a technique to focus your studying so that you're aware of your strengths and improve on weak areas. To use KWL, begin by writing everything you know or think you know (K) about the topic. Then, draw a line on your paper to separate these ideas from the next step. Now, write down what you want to learn (W) or need to learn about the topic. You can use your notes, questions asked by your instructor or other students in class, or your test review to help you with this step. Next, you need to find some answers. You can consult your notes, your textbook, classmates, returned assignments, or your instructor. Finally, draw a line to create the last section and write down what you learned (L). You may find that you thought you knew something when you wrote it down under the K category, only to find out that you were wrong. Write out what you learned. By using this technique, you confirm previous knowledge, clarify concepts, and gain new insight.

STUDENT NOTES

KWL Example

K: What do I know about organizing a paper?

- Need a thesis, which is the main point you're making
- Start with introduction
- Each ¶ needs a topic sentence
- Must have three body paragraphs

W: What do I want or need to know about organizing a paper?

- What's a good way to start the paper (intro)?
- What's the relationship between the topic sentence and the thesis? (instructor question in class)

L: What did I learn about organizing a paper?

- <u>Intro</u> should grab reader's attention. Try using a story, interesting statistic or fact, hypothetical situation, or quote.
- Actually, don't have to have 3 <u>body paragraphs</u>. Just make sure body ¶ order makes sense logically & that you have enough body ¶ to support your thesis.
- <u>Conclusion</u> shouldn't just rehash: Should bring readers out from talking about very specific pts. to larger context.
- <u>Topic Sentences</u> support the thesis. Group similar ideas and find their common element to write TS.
- Don't forget <u>transitions</u> between ¶

Remember, between the W and L stages, you must do some research to find the answers to your questions and to confirm what you think you know about the topic (K category).

What myth did this student debunk for himself by using KWL?

Record your goals for incorporating specific study strategies into your study routines on the tracking sheet on page 85 for easy reference in the future.

Conclusion

Students have many misconceptions when it comes to studying. They often assume studying means to sit passively staring at the book open in front of them. However, just like you learned about reading in Chapter 6, you must be active when studying if you are to engage enough with the ideas to understand them and commit them to memory. Color-coding your notes, making flash cards, creating Venn diagrams, writing a creative mnemonic device, drawing a concept map, working sample problems, creating a practice test, reviewing returned work, writing an informal outline, creating a cheat sheet, presenting to your study group, and using KWL are all study actions that lead to a better understanding of material. Finding the most effective studying strategies requires you to consider your learning preferences and the type of material presented. It will also require some time and patience, as well as the realization that studying is an ongoing process throughout the semester, not just in the few days or hours leading up to a test.

Study Strategies Troubleshooting

Problem	Solution
Not remembering specific, detailed information	• Complete problem sets or practice in the book. • Make flash cards for specific terms, dates, formulas, or processes. Use the mitosis example on page 144 to help. • Make an acrostic sentence or mnemonic.
Not remembering major themes or overarching ideas	• Form a study group. By identifying the main concepts to be divided amongst the group, you'll know the key areas and concepts to keep in mind. • Create a practice test, specifically focusing on possible essay choices. • Review the questions at the end of chapters, especially short answer or essay questions that include the terms "why" or "how." • Create flash cards similar to the Bay of Pigs example on page 144.
Losing focus or getting bored when studying	• Utilize the study strategies that are well-matched for visual or kinesthetic learners, such as making flash cards, color-coding your notes, or creating visual diagrams. • Look for videos of class concepts on YouTube. You'll be shocked at what is available. Just remember to consider the reliability of the source in selecting your video.
Cramming at the last minute	• Don't forget to complete maintenance studying. • Use your planner to devote specific times to complete particular study tasks. For example, between your two Monday morning classes, will you run through your computer science class flash cards twice or will you create a Venn diagram for history class? See Chapter 5 for more time-management strategies.
Not knowing how to prepare for a test or exam	• Look at the learning outcomes as well as the outline of instruction in the syllabus for topics to study. • Work with a study group to identify important material or themes.

STUDENT NOTES

CHAPTER 8
Study Strategies

1. What three things cause students to not study effectively?

2. Label each of the 11 study methods on pages 143–154 as either Maintenance or Preparation. Compare your answers to a classmate's.

3. Examine the differences between the Venn diagram, outline, and concept map. Which of these do you find most helpful? In what ways do they help you?

4. Both PEMDAS and Please Excuse My Dear Aunt Sally help people remember the order of operations in math class.

   a. Which of these is an acronym?

   b. Which one is an acrostic sentence?

   c. Which helps you the most?

5. Now that Pluto has been stripped of its status as a planet, a new acrostic sentence needs to be created to help students remember the order of the planets. Create a suggestion.

6. What study technique did you learn about that you will now try to use when studying? How do you think it will help you?

7. Ryan passed all of his high school classes without opening a book. Now, he is in his first semester and is taking four classes: MAT 152 (Statistics), ENG 111 (Writing and Inquiry), COM 231 (Public Speaking), and BIO 111 (General Biology). He doesn't know how to even begin to study for his classes because he did not have to study in high school. What advice can you give him for studying effectively for those subjects? Identify at least one unique maintenance strategy for each subject.

8. Roger is an older student who has been out of the classroom for almost a decade. He is currently taking CHM 151 (General Chemistry I). In his Chemistry class, the instructor does not give quizzes, homework assignments, or lab grades. Instead, students take only two tests and a final exam. Roger is extremely nervous about the upcoming first test of the semester. He has joined a study group, but the other students get distracted easily and just make Roger more nervous. In fact, Roger is thinking about dropping the course and taking another science next semester. What advice can you give him for preparing for his upcoming test? Identify at least three strategies.

Test-Taking Strategies

The first step in doing well on a test is mastering the content. The previous chapters in this unit described many effective ways of doing this: reading strategically, studying with effective methods, managing your time to ensure you allow yourself the time to learn, and taking good notes. Using these methods should be your priority in preparing for a test. However, there are some additional important strategies to keep in mind for the test itself, categorized by time and the type of test.

◻ Before the Test

Nip test anxiety in the bud before the day of the test by using effective study methods. Many students say they are bad test takers when their difficulties are actually a result of ineffective studying. Their text anxiety comes from knowing they are unprepared for the test or from feeling woefully unprepared as they read and attempt to answer the test questions. Consider if this describes your experiences in test taking. If so, review the study strategies in Chapter 8. It might be a good idea to create a short-term SMART goal for your test anxiety to see if using studying methods can help you overcome your test anxiety. Preparing adequately for your tests and setting goals to minimize your anxiety should help you overcome test anxiety. However, if test anxiety continues to distract you, consult with a counselor in the Counseling and Student Development office to learn of other strategies to help you.

If necessary, change your behaviors in order to avoid the Nervous Nellies. Keep your distance from these students who tend to get worked up before the test and feed off each others' nervous energy. This group of students often ends up psyching each other out or building their anxiety levels by complaining about the test, discussing what will be on the test at the last minute (when there's not enough time to study if they did forget something), and otherwise causing negative anticipation for the test. Keep your distance by waiting down the hall before the test.

Make sure you clarify the testing method with the instructor several days in advance. It would be devastating to prepare for a multiple choice test, only to receive the test and find it is mostly short answer and essays. It's also a good idea to talk about time expectations. Will the test take the entire class period? Will the test be timed?

When studying specifically for a test, make sure you review your notes for any questions the instructor posed during class. These will likely appear on the test. Prepare yourself for the exam by sketching out possible answers to short answer or essay questions the instructor will likely repeat on the test.

If there are still a couple of concepts you're not completely confident about, you may want to write final reminders on an index card to review one or two more times on test day. In effect, you're creating a cheat sheet, which is one of the study methods discussed in Chapter 8. Of course, you won't use this card during the test, but creating the card will help you remember this tough material and also ease your nerves because you know exactly what to review one last time.

Also, try to reduce the potential for last-minute panicking. Make sure you have all your materials before the test, so you won't be scrambling for a pencil or calculator. It's a good idea to check your bag the night before the test to make sure you have the supplies you need to perform well.

On test day, plan to arrive to campus early. The last thing you want is to add to your normal stress levels by panicking about the time or becoming frustrated with traffic. Set your alarm for an earlier time and take the earlier bus or leave home 15 minutes early.

Further prepare yourself for the test by planning your behaviors on test day. Create a mantra, or positive statement, to repeat to yourself when you begin to experience anxiety. For example, when you feel yourself becoming nervous, you could inhale deeply and say to yourself, "I've prepared for this test. I will do well. I will be fine." Exhale slowly and repeat until you feel more peaceful.

Also plan to sit away from others, even if this means you do not sit in your regular seat. If you are usually distracted when others get up to turn in their tests or leave early, make sure you sit far away from the door or the place where students submit tests. This will minimize the extent of the distractions.

During the Test

As soon as you are allowed to begin, immediately write down formulas, mnemonic devices (see page 150 in Chapter 8), or specific dates or names you're afraid you'll forget. This method, called a **mind dump**, will allow you to concentrate on the test rather than on remembering.

After you've written down this information, write your name on the test materials and then **survey** the test. Look over the exam to determine its length and which sections are worth the most points. Then, decide how you will budget your time effectively to get the most points. Will you begin with the essay on the last page? Should you start with the identifications in the middle of the test? Surveying the test and planning your test strategy should take no more than two to three minutes.

Make sure you don't foolishly give away points by failing to read the directions. Students often skip the directions out of nervousness and haste. However, this can be a very costly mistake. When reading the directions, annotate them by marking verbs (for example, *match, consider, evaluate, circle, define, compare and contrast*) and any other words that stand out to you in the instructions. Make sure you know your task before you write in any answers. If your instructor has asked you to compare and contrast two events, discussing just the similarities will cause you to lose points. Sometimes questions can have multiple answers or contain important words such as *except, not,* or *without*. Underline these important stipulations or risk losing points.

As you move through the test, consider the type of question you're answering. You'll approach a multiple-choice question much differently than you will an essay prompt or a true/false question. Be mindful of the types of answers expected for specific question types as well as common mistakes students make. Read the "Types of Test Questions" section on pages 163–171 for specific information about question types.

You should also be careful to clearly mark your answers. Do not assume the instructor will know what your answer should be. Mark your answers as indicated in the instructions. If you erase, do so thoroughly and rewrite your answer so that it is clear and not difficult to read. When writing in your answers for multiple choice and true/false questions, make sure your letters are clear. Instructors will not assume what you meant by the dreaded T/F hybrid answer (a T that also has the lowest bar of the F, shown below). It's best to be overly clear rather than to lose points because your answer is ambiguous or illegible. Erase your previous answer and consider writing out the word "true" or "false" if your answer is still not clear. Be obvious or risk losing points.

F

You will encounter some difficulties when proceeding through the test but don't be thrown off course. If you find yourself feeling anxious, focus on the positive. For example, take a moment to acknowledge the number of questions you did know or the areas of the test for which you feel very confident. Realize that you're feeling stress, which is often a result of doubt. To counteract this negative feeling, state the opposite to yourself through your mantra: "I've prepared for this test. I am doing well. I will be fine." Exhale slowly and repeat until you feel more peaceful.

If you're feeling stuck because you do not know an answer, fall back on the **two-pass method** of test taking. On the first pass, you work straight through the test, from the beginning of the test through to the last questions. When you encounter a question you don't know, quickly put an answer for the question (if it's essay or short answer, jot down some quick notes) just in case you run out of time on the test. But make sure you also mark that question by circling the number or by placing a question mark in the margin. Before you turn in your test or before time is called, take a second pass through the test and look at the questions you marked as uncertain answers. Did you remember anything during the rest of the test that can help you recall the answer? Did anything on the latter part of the test provide you with the answer? Change your response if necessary.

While taking the test, also be mindful of the time. Being mindful is not the same as worrying. Mindfulness means that you periodically check the classroom clock or your watch to ensure your plan for completing the test is on track.

Remember, certain sections of the test are often worth more points than other sections. Usually high-point value areas are short-answer questions or essays, which tend to appear toward the end of the test. You don't want to run out of time before you get to the big points, so make sure you keep track of time by knowing the end time of the test and watching the classroom clock. You can also complete these questions first, if you'd like.

Finally, check over your test before you submit it. Never leave questions blank. If you had a 50% chance of picking the correct lottery numbers, you would play, right? The same goes for true/false questions. For true/false questions, you have a 50% chance of getting the answer right, so take a guess. For multiple-choice and matching questions, your odds are also favorable. Make an educated guess and move on. For essay or short-answer questions, aim for partial points by writing down what you do know. If pressed for time, still leave one to two minutes at the end of the test before time is called to mark answers to true/false or multiple-choice questions that you haven't gotten to yet.

After the Test

If you studied effectively and did your best, you should reward yourself and do something that brings you joy as a reward. For example, you could go see the movie you've been putting off because you were studying or you could get a nice lunch and sit outside for a picnic.

After you've treated yourself, evaluate your studying and test-taking strategies. How well did your methods work? In what ways were you well prepared? What could you do differently next time in order to perform better on the test? It's very important that you attend the class meeting during which your instructor will return the test, which is often the next class, so that you'll have the opportunity to review your work. When the instructor returns your test, don't just look at your grade or what you missed. Also consider how your studying or test-taking methods helped or hurt your score. Examine your test to learn from your mistakes.

Types of Test Questions

In addition to considering how you'll proceed through testing, you should think strategically about the tasks you'll be presented with during the test. Your approach and considerations should differ based on the question type.

Multiple Choice

Multiple-choice questions present a question and several possible answers. Your task is to select the best possible answer from the list, which is usually represented by a letter. Most often, there is only one response or letter that correctly answers the question. Here's an example:

> 1. Students desiring to take classes at a community college and then transfer to a four-year institution have how many options?
>   a. None
>   b. One
>   c. Three
>   d. Four
>   e. Unlimited

Review Chapter 2 for the answer to this question.

Multiple-choice questions are common on college tests, although they rarely comprise the entire test. Many students erroneously believe multiple-choice questions to be the easiest section of the test. While it is true that your chances of selecting the correct answer are usually 1 in 4 or 1 in 5, it's doubtful that most students would be content with a 20% or 25% on the test! You should not shirk preparation studying just because a test is mainly multiple choice.

If you regularly miss multiple-choice questions, consider if your preparation (reading or studying) is part of the problem. If not, the likely culprit is the method you use to answer multiple-choice questions. The main problem that students encounter with multiple-choice tests is that they do not come up with their own answer to the question before looking at the answer choices. Unfortunately, once you read the answer choices, you cannot get those options or their wording out of your head. The test author's words may confuse you even when you know the answer, so make sure you use the following four-step process to avoid the common pitfalls of multiple choice tests. You're less likely to be influenced by false answers if you use this four-step technique.

Four-Step Process to Answering Multiple-Choice Questions
1. First, cover up the answer choices so you won't be swayed by them. You can use your hand, the answer sheet, or scrap paper if it's allowed.
2. Then, read the question. Annotate its important parts, including words such as *not*, *without*, *only*, or *except*. Students often miss these words when reading the question.
3. Next, formulate your own answer to the test question. Without the distraction of answers that "sound" good, you're more likely to be able to find the correct answer.
4. Finally, uncover the answer choices and use the process of elimination, or POE. To do this, don't read the answer choices looking for the answer that most nearly matches yours from step 3. Instead, look for the wrong answers to eliminate. If the answers provided don't match your own answer, mark them out. The one that's left must be the right answer. Evaluate if it is indeed the one that most closely matches your own answer (keep in mind it might not be an exact match). Select this answer.

Consider the following example and the chemistry student's process for answering the question. Before reading this question, the student covered up answer choices **a** through **d**. She then read the question and considered what she knew about inert gases and their most important characteristics. She then jotted down a few notes in the margin. Finally, she uncovered the answer choices and eliminated any options that did not match her notes or that contradicted her list. After this process, the only choice left is answer **c**, which has to be the best answer.

> *Inert means doesn't move or react*
> *Nitrogen is in experiments b/c it doesn't*
> *react and can be controlled*
>
> 2. Which of the following is an important or defining characteristic of inert gases?
>   a. ~~Inert gases oxidize.~~
>   b. ~~Inert gases react strongly to chemicals.~~
>   c. The valence of inert gases is complete.
>   d. ~~Inert gases cannot be controlled in experiments.~~

Another reason students often miss multiple-choice questions is that they do not look at all the answer choices. Make sure you evaluate all answer choices, even if answer choice **a** seems to be correct. Remember, you're not looking for the right answer; you're looking for wrong answers to eliminate. By evaluating all the answer choices, you'll also avoid a common error, which is marking answer **a** when the answer is not only **a**. See the example below to understand.

> 3. Which of the following is true?
>   a. An infinitive contains the word "to" and the unconjugated verb
>   b. Verbs only need to agree in tense with the rest of the sentence
>   c. Verbs should match their subjects in numbers (plural verbs with multiple subjects; singular verbs with single subjects)
>   d. All of the above
>   e. Both a and c

While answer choice **a** is a factual statement, so is answer choice **c**. You must read through all of the answer choices to see that answer choice **e** is the correct answer for this item because it includes statements **a** and **c**.

While nothing beats knowing the content of the test, when you're confused on a multiple-choice question, consider the following strategies:

■ **Look for answer choices that are opposites of each other.** One of these is likely the correct answer.

> 4. Which of the following is true of the larynx?
>   a. It is open during swallowing.
>   b. It is 4–5 inches long.
>   c. It is closed during swallowing.
>   d. It extends from the soft palate to the epiglottis.

Answer choices **a** and **c** are opposites: either the larynx is open or it is closed during swallowing. Therefore, the answer is likely either **a** or **c**.

■   **Avoid picking the correct answer to the wrong question.** Just because an answer choice is a true statement doesn't mean that it correctly answers the question asked. Make sure your answer choice is not only true but actually responds to the posed prompt.

> 5.   Why did the pilgrims come to America?
>   a.   To avoid religious persecution in their native country.
>   b.   King James succeeded Queen Elizabeth.
>   c.   The pilgrims founded New England.
>   d.   Because they wanted to eat a Thanksgiving meal.

Answers **a**, **b**, and **c** are factually correct. However, only **a** answers the question and is a historically valid reason why the pilgrims came to the Americas.

■   **Avoid picking answers with absolutes.** Answers with the extreme words *every, all, totally, completely, only, none, never,* and *always* do not allow for exceptions, and in reality there are exceptions to nearly every rule. Therefore, answers containing these words are rarely correct. Instead, if you're stuck between two answers, look for the one that contains qualifiers, such as *usually, most, some, rarely, nearly, almost,* and *often* since these words allow for exceptions to the rules.

> 6.   Pavlov's theory on classical conditioning can be best described as...
>   a.   A theory that only applies to experiments with dogs.
>   b.   Always applies to food responses.
>   c.   Usually describes a behavior learned through the simultaneous presence of conditioned and unconditioned stimuli.
>   d.   Supported by behaviorists, such as Bandura.

Surprisingly, you don't need to know anything about Pavlov or classical conditioning to narrow down the answer choices. Eliminate answer choices with extreme answers and then consider the answers with qualifiers. Answer choices **a** and **b** have extreme words (*only* and *always*), so mark them out. Now you're left with **c** and **d**. If you knew nothing else of Pavlov's theory and the answer choices, you should mark answer choice **c** as correct since it contains conditional language (*usually*).

True/False

True/False questions usually present a statement that the test taker must evaluate and mark as being a factual statement (true) or an inaccurate statement (false). Many students dread true/false questions because they become confused or find the questions tricky. Use the following two strategies to help you overcome the feeling that the questions were intended to mislead you.

Remember that if part of the answer is false, then the entire answer is false. Divide the sentence into phrases and place check marks above what is true and an X over any part that is untrue. If you place an X over any part of the sentence, then the answer cannot be true. Mark it false.

> 7. Shakespeare, a well-known poet and playwright, is often thought
>
> of as the greatest American author.

Should statement 7 be marked as true or false?

Also, as with multiple-choice entries, avoid marking statements containing absolutes as true—or consider absolutes very carefully. Since most things in life do have exceptions, answer choices without conditions will often be false. The word *always* in item 8 below should make you wary of marking this answer as true.

> 8. The law of demand states that the quantity and price demanded in a given market are always in an inverse relationship.

Matching

Matching questions are usually presented in two columns. The test taker is to match the terms (usually in the left column) to the definition or characteristics presented (usually in the right column). These question types can be deceptively hard. To avoid common matching errors, make sure you've read the directions. Sometimes answers can match more than one term or question.

Also, examine the columns presented for matching. Do you understand the task at hand? Find a systematic way to go about answering the questions. Often it is easiest to work your way through the right-hand column (usually the explanations for the terms in the left column) and find corresponding terms on the left rather than vice versa. Do not draw lines to match items.

This is confusing and wastes time. Pair items mentally and then write the corresponding letter or number next to the question or term.

Don't forget to use the process of elimination (POE). Match the ones you know most certainly first and mark off the answers you've used. Then concentrate on the remaining choices.

1. _____ benefactor		a.	a kind or generous act
2. _____ benediction		b.	something advantageous or good
3. _____ benefit		c.	a person who donates time or money
4. _____ benevolent		d.	a blessing
5. _____ beneficial		e.	helpful

Rather than read through the answers in the right column to find the answer for a term on the left, begin with reading **a** in the right column and then find its answer on the left. Using this method requires less reading and is less time-consuming than the traditional method.

Fill in the Blank

Fill-in-the-blank questions provide a sentence in which one or more words are replaced with a space for the test taker to insert the term or phrase that will complete the statement or make it true. Usually, the instructor intends for you to provide a specific term, list of steps, date, or number when answering a fill-in-the-blank question.

> 9. The _____ connects the end of the ulna to the end of the radius and helps the pronator teres rotate the arm inside.

The instructor expects the student to provide a specific term in the blank. To answer these question types, think back to bolded words in the book, terms the instructor wrote on the board (the O of SOARS in Chapter 7), or terms your instructor repeated in class (the R or S of SOARS in Chapter 7). By visualizing the list of words, dates, or steps, you may be more likely to recall them, especially if your learning style relies heavily on visual stimuli to learn (see Chapter 1 for more information about learning styles). Look at the answer choices to other questions, especially multiple choice if they are on the test. However, be forewarned that fill-in-the-blank questions are the hardest to use strategy to solve if you don't know the answer. If you don't know the answer, you'll likely not receive credit since the instructor probably wants a particular term or date. Nevertheless, you can write an explanation of the term in the blank or write what you do know. You may receive some partial credit.

Short Answer

Short-answer questions require a brief written response. The length expectation can vary from one word to a phrase to several concise sentences, so make sure you read the directions and consult with your instructor if you're unclear how much to write. You don't want to spend excessive time on short-answer questions if your instructor only expected a few brief phrases. Here's an example of a short-answer question.

> 10. Define and explain the following terms by describing important features, contributions, or legacies. Write no more than four sentences for each.
>   • Federalist Party
>   • War of 1812
>   • John Marshall

Short-answer questions tend to worry many students. To get the most points possible, do your best to be exact and concise with your answers. If the short answer requires an identification (like the example above), make sure you include all relevant points by writing an answer that addresses all of the question words: *who, what, when, where, how,* and *why.* You don't want to risk not getting points when you knew the information but didn't write it down. Before you move on, ask yourself if you answered all of the question words related to the topic.

If you can't recall the correct answer, don't dwell on this. Instead of concentrating on what you don't know, concentrate on what you do know. Write down this information in the space for the answer. Partial credit is better than no credit at all.

Essay

Essay questions usually provide a prompt or question that students answer in one or more paragraphs. Essay questions require not only knowledge of the content, but also a clear understanding of the question, effective organization, and succinct writing. To lessen the stress associated with essay questions, read the question carefully and circle any verbs in the essay so that you'll understand your assigned task. For example, are you to explain, compare and contrast, analyze, or describe? Also, you should make sure you know exactly what topics you are to cover. You may want to underline these. Are you to discuss a person, her achievements, or her legacy? You should be clear about your job before you begin or risk losing significant points. Always annotate the prompt. The following prompt has been annotated to clarify the assignment and the student's responsibilities before he begins brainstorming.

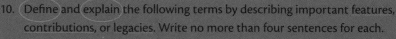

10. Define and explain the following terms by describing important features, contributions, or legacies. Write no more than four sentences for each.
- Federalist Party
- War of 1812
- John Marshall

After you annotate an essay prompt to gain a clear understanding of what's being asked, you should then recall all of your knowledge that could help you answer the questions. Write down what you know on the topic, so you can focus on what you do know rather than stressing about what you don't know. In other words, brainstorm in the margin or on scrap paper. If you get stuck, you may be able to flip through other parts of the test to refresh your memory.

After gathering your ideas, sketch an outline. If you don't have a plan for your essay, you'll likely stray off-topic. Also, you don't have time or space to revise your essay significantly. Taking a few minutes to write down a rough outline and thesis will pay off with more points in the end. It's a step well worth your time.

With your outline in hand, begin writing. Incorporate relevant specific points, names, dates, and terms to demonstrate your knowledge. Refer to the brainstormed list of what you do know for ideas. Periodically check back with the prompt as you're writing. Again, make sure you are answering the question that's being asked.

Scantrons or Bubble Sheets

Many students make errors on Scantron or bubble sheets, giving away points when they know the correct answers to the questions because they incorrectly mark their answers or do not thoroughly erase. You may not even realize that this is a problem for you since many Scantrons are used for final exams and often you do not have the opportunity to review your Scantron sheet for errors since the class is over.

To avoid losing points because of incomplete erasures—a common problem—write your answers on the test and only bubble in your selected answer either after you finish an entire page of the test or at the end of the test. This will prevent erasures due to changing your mind on an answer (because you won't bubble in answers until you're finished with the test itself) and will also prevent getting off a line when going back and forth after every question. Students give away points unnecessarily by accidentally skipping lines when going back and forth between the test and the answer sheet. This method of test taking—reading a question, deciding on the answer, marking the answer on the Scantron, and then going back to the test to re-peat the process—is also time-consuming. Students lose valuable time going back and forth from the test to the answer sheet. To solve this problem, use the suggested method, so you're only moving back and forth from the test to the answer sheet at the end of the test page or at the end of the test. Also bubble answers in sets of three. It's much easier, less confusing, and also time-saving to remember and bubble A-C-A and then D-B-A rather than to go back and forth for each answer (A, bubble, back to test, C, bubble, back to test, A, bubble back to test, D, bubble, back to test, etc.).

Conclusion

Students often remark that they're either good or bad test takers, as if one's performance on a test is a matter of an inherent trait that you're either born with or without. However, test taking is a skill that can be improved, and this fact may be perhaps the most important thing to remember about test taking. All test takers can improve their performances on tests with atten-tion to their approach and knowledge of tests themselves.

> Record your personal test-taking goals on the tracking sheet on page 85 for easy reference in the future.

Remember that instructors utilize tests in order to gauge how well stu-dents have mastered important course content. Since tests are designed to measure how well you know the material, the first steps of quality test preparation begin with good study and reading habits (see Chapters 6 and 8). Beyond knowing the content, you'll also need to prepare for the specific testing method. Remember, various types of test questions will require dif-ferent kinds of preparation studying (see Chapter 8), so knowing the format and length of each test is critical to being able to show your knowledge.

When you have an important test coming up, decide on a three-part strat-egy: what you'll do before the test, during the test, and after the test. Will you utilize the two-pass method? What items will you write down as a mind dump? How will you keep track of and manage your time? How will you keep in mind the expectations of the question type to make sure you're including the kinds of information necessary to receive the most points? Finally, how will you learn from your mistakes to become a better test taker in the future? When it comes to successful test taking, preparing for the test itself is just as important as learning the material. Without either, you will not be able to demonstrate the full extent of your knowledge or abilities.

Test-Taking Troubleshooting

Problems	Solutions
Freezing on a test due to anxiety or your mind going blank	• Look at the rest of the test. Other content can trigger your memory. • Repeat your mantra. • Resolve to study better next time. Review Chapter 8 and adopt two or three new study strategies for the next test. • Change your test day game plan. Don't interact with Nervous Nellies, and sit away from distractions.
Running out of time on a test	• Sit where you can see the clock or wear a watch. Survey the test and then budget time for each section. • Prioritize points. If you cannot finish the test, go to the questions worth the most points and concentrate on answering those well. • A minute or two before the end of the test, turn to T/F or matching questions you have not completed and guess. • Use the two-pass method so you don't get hung up and use time unproductively. Concentrate on getting all the points you can by answering the ones you know first. Star or circle questions you don't know. Go back to them after you've finished answering the ones you know.
Missing questions when you know the answer	• Read questions carefully. Make sure you underline important terms such as *except*, *not*, and *least*. • Make sure you are marking your Scantron correctly. • Consider the question types and the tips for responding to each. • Pace yourself so that you have time to complete the test.

CHAPTER 9
Test-Taking Strategies

1. Look at the list of things you should do before you take a test. Which of these do you usually do? Which could you do better? Which ones do you need to add to your routine?

2. Which test format (multiple choice, true/false, fill-in-the-blank, short answer, essay) causes you the most anxiety? What will you do to improve your test taking for these types of questions?

3. Annotate this sample essay question prompt as you should when you take an exam. Mark the most important terms to keep in mind when responding to the prompt.

> In a three-paragraph essay, identify three causes of the American Civil War other than slavery and explain how each led to secession.

4. Use the strategies discussed in this chapter to practice your test-taking skills on the practice test below. Don't worry, you don't need to know anything about the topics to be able to answer the questions. The answers follow.

Practice Test

Directions: Circle your answer.

1. True or False: Marsupials are only found in Australia.

2. True or False: Most diesel engines use a two-way catalytic converter.

3. True or False: Electrons are always lighter in mass than protons.

4. Which of the following is a city in Ghana?
    a. Sunyani
    b. Chapel Hill
    c. Durham
    d. Raleigh

5. Which of the following songs was not recorded by Michael Jackson?
    a. "Thriller"
    b. "Poker Face"
    c. "Billie Jean"
    d. Both A and C

---

5. Sofia is new to the college, new to North Carolina, new to the United States. She has a college degree from her native country, but has enrolled to pursue a new career. In her country, the only tests that students take are essay exams and oral exams. Before Sofia came to the U.S., she had never taken a multiple-choice or true/false test. So far this semester, Sofia has not made good grades on her tests even though she felt like she knew the material that the tests covered. What advice can you offer Sofia to help her succeed with these particular testing formats?

6. Kathy hasn't been in school for almost twenty years, and in her first semester back she's very concerned about taking quizzes, tests, and exams since it's been so long since she has taken one. In her PSY 150 (General Psychology) class, 20% of her grade comes from quizzes and 40% from the three unit tests. She's taken two quizzes so far, failing one and barely passing the other. Her first unit test is coming up in two weeks, and Kathy thinks that if she doesn't do well, she might drop the class. What three things from this chapter would you share with Kathy if she turned to you for help as a classmate?

Practice Test Answers:

1. False. Remember that the use of extreme words such as "only" often indicates that the question is false.

2. True. Words like "most"—instead of extreme words like "all" or "every"—often indicate a correct answer.

3. True. Yes, sometimes extreme words can be used in a true/false statement and the answer is still true. Remember, nothing should replace first knowing the course content!

4. This question illustrates that looking for the wrong answers to eliminate—instead of searching for the right answer—will help you on multiple choice tests. While you may have never heard of the city of Sunyani, it was reasonable for you to assume that our local town names would not be names of cities in a country whose official languages do not include English.

5. You need to know a little bit about pop culture to get the answer to this one correct. If you marked A, C, or D, was it because you did not read the question carefully enough to see the word "not"? If so, make sure you read and annotate your questions before answering.

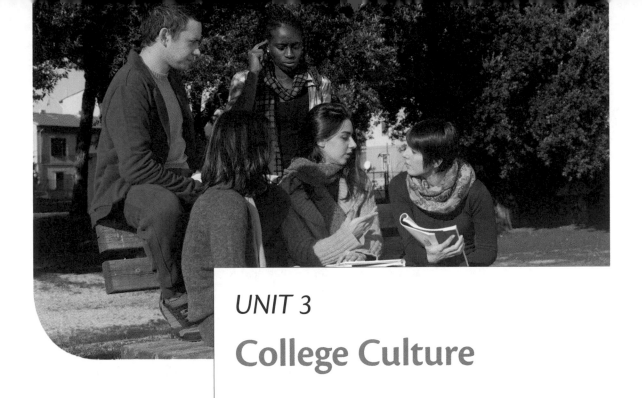

UNIT 3
College Culture

To fully understand how to participate in the scholarly community of a specific institution of higher education, you have to understand the culture of the institution. College culture includes more than just knowing where different offices are on campus. You must be able to speak the language, observe the cultural norms, and navigate the systems. Many students experience "culture shock" in their first semester because college is so different from what they experienced in high school or because it has been a long time since they've been in a classroom environment. The chapters in this unit will help prevent you from suffering from "culture shock" at your community college.

You can learn a lot about the culture of a particular college or university by reading its mission statement. The North Carolina Community College System mission statement is excerpted below from its website (http://www.nccommunitycolleges.edu, accessed February 20, 2014):

"The mission of the North Carolina Community College System is to open the door to high-quality, accessible educational opportunities that minimize barriers to post-secondary education, maximize student success, develop a globally and multi-culturally competent workforce, and improve the lives and well-being of individuals by providing:

- Education, training and retraining for the workforce including basic skills and literacy education, occupational and pre-baccalaureate programs.

- Support for economic development through services to and in partnership with business and industry and in collaboration with the University of North Carolina System and private colleges and universities.

■ Services to communities and individuals which improve the quality of life."

Look for your college's mission on its website or in the college catalog to learn more about the college's values and how it perceives its role in your community. You'll likely find some of the same concepts (for example, supporting student success, providing a qualified workforce, offering a variety of levels of instruction to adults) as you see in the system-wide mission above.

Chapter 10 College Student Roles and Responsibilities

In order to move successfully through a culture, you must know what behaviors are appropriate and inappropriate. It should be obvious to you by now that you can't assume that successful navigation of high school will automatically prepare you for the college environment. This chapter highlights many of the expectations that most community colleges have of their students.

Chapter 11 The College Community

As you become familiar with your different roles as a college student, you may seek help from the college in fulfilling those expectations. Chapter 11 describes many of the most valuable resources on campus for new college students as well as tips for using them effectively. Again, see the college website for updates and additional resources.

Important Learning Outcomes for Unit 3:

- Explain the rights and responsibilities of a college student and an advisee.

- Identify essential college policies and procedures, including academic integrity, avoiding plagiarism; calculating a GPA; and maintaining satisfactory academic progress for financial aid eligibility and/or good academic standing.

- Identify essential college resources, including financial aid, advising, registration, tutoring, library services, computer labs, and counseling services and recognize the importance of these resources on student success.

Unit 3: College Culture Tracking Sheet

As you read Unit 3, record the individual elements of your personal college culture in the table below. This will be a helpful record to track your personalized preferences and plans.

Advisor Contact Information	Student Clubs or Organizations that Interest You
Instructional Delivery Formats that Match Your Learning Preferences	**Two College Departments or Services to Explore Further**
Cumulative GPA Goal	**Program GPA Goal**

STUDENT NOTES

College Student Roles and Responsibilities

E ntering college after high school or after time in the workforce can be a surprisingly difficult adjustment for some students. For one thing, college expectations are very different from high school expectations.

In high school, the teacher is frequently in charge of students' learning. The high school teacher often provides regular opportunities for students to check their understanding with graded homework and chapter tests or quizzes. The high school teacher also gives regular reminders of upcoming deadlines and tests and may devote significant time in class to helping students prepare for assignments and tests. Also, high schools often have strict policies (for example, government-mandated attendance until the age of 16), but there are important variations in the policies (for example, a differentiation between excused and unexcused absences).

In college, on the other hand, learning is often self-directed. College instructors facilitate fewer in-class opportunities for students to check their understanding. College students may have to take fewer tests, and the individual test grades will count significantly more toward their overall grade in the class. For example, you may take only four tests in one class, and each test may cover up to five textbook chapters and several weeks of classroom instruction. Likewise, college homework is rarely graded; college instructors often just assume that students see the value of the homework and that students have completed it before class. Completing college homework is often part of the maintenance studying you learned about in Chapter 8. The payoff for doing homework in college comes when you are well prepared for class, you are learning the material at the pace set by the instructor, and you do well on your tests. Finally, college policies can also seem strict, and they are applied to all students with fewer exceptions (for example, excused absences in college are very rare).

Therefore, it is in your best interest to familiarize yourself with the roles and responsibilities you fulfill as a college student, including classroom and campus policies and how your work is evaluated. This chapter will introduce you to several tools that will help you understand your roles and your responsibilities as a college student, so you can be a successful college student.

▢ Expectations of College Students

The introduction to this chapter described some of the key differences between high school and college and how those differences impact college students' roles and responsibilities. For example, college students are expected to attend and fully participate in every class meeting, come to class prepared, and advocate for themselves when they need additional support for their learning.

Specifically, college instructors expect students to contribute to the day's lesson by thoughtfully completing the assigned readings and homework before class. While it is possible to be successful in many high school settings by doing your homework on the bus on the way to school or during another class, these habits will not lead to success in college. Your college instructors expect that you are spending two hours outside of class for every one hour in class. This level of dedication to your education cannot be met if you throw together homework assignments at the last minute or skim textbook chapters that you should have read more carefully. Sometimes, students expect their instructors to provide an overview of reading assignments and homework during class. Many college instructors will not provide such an overview; instead they will use class time to build upon the concepts introduced in the reading assignments and homework. When you prepare appropriately for class, you can then completely participate in discussions and group activities. This participation will help you pay attention during class and will help you understand the course content.

Another common expectation of college students is that you monitor your own learning and seek help when you need it. College instructors rarely give weekly quizzes to check students' comprehension of the small details of the class. Instead, college instructors expect students to keep up with the class instruction by completing homework as discussed above and by actively participating in class. In addition to paying attention and taking notes, successful college students also ask their instructors to clarify and/or elaborate on confusing concepts. You should know how you learn best and then find the resources that will help you succeed in each of your classes. For example, if you have a strong preference for a visual learning style, and your instructor uses lecture exclusively, then you should ask your instructor about visual resources you can use to enhance your classroom learning. See Chapter 1 for more examples of how to make your learning style preferences work for you.

It is appropriate to have certain expectations of your college instructors, too. You can expect your college instructors to be well prepared for class, to start and end class on time (using the full period of instruction each week), and to fully explain the course learning outcomes and each assignment's learning outcomes. Notice the emphasis on the reciprocity of the expectations of college students and faculty. For example, students are expected to arrive on time, and faculty are expected to begin class on time. Students are expected to seek help when they need it, and faculty are expected to be available to students outside of class.

Your college instructors are experts in their fields and dedicated educators. They take their responsibilities very seriously, and they have high expectations of you as an adult learner. If you adequately demonstrate your dedication to your education through regular attendance, participation in class, using out-of-class resources (including office hours and tutorial services), then your instructors will do their best to help you succeed in their classes.

How to Use a Syllabus

The class **syllabus** is the most important handout your instructor will give you all semester. Your instructor will likely discuss the syllabus on the first day of class, but you should read the syllabus very carefully after class, so you'll know exactly what to expect in a specific class. Each instructor organizes the information in her syllabus differently, but you can typically find the following very useful information in every college syllabus: instructor contact information, class policies, and an outline of instruction.

The class syllabus will list your **instructor's contact information**, including her telephone number, email address, office location, and office hours. Your instructor will likely have an office on campus but not necessarily in the same building as your classroom. If your instructor is a part-time college employee, then she may not have an office on campus; however, you should still be able to call or email the instructor for out-of-class assistance. All full-time instructors and many part-time instructors dedicate a specific amount of time each week to working with students outside of class. This time is called **office hours**, and it is your opportunity to connect with your instructors beyond the classroom. Most instructors prefer for students to make an appointment to see them even during office hours. Sometimes instructors are meeting with other students or have to be called away from the office unexpectedly, so an appointment will help guarantee that your instructor is in the office and available to you during a convenient time.

Your syllabus will also include **important class policies**, for example, the attendance, withdrawal, late work, and grading policies. The attendance policy will indicate whether or not you will receive a grade for your attendance

Five reasons to visit your instructor during office hours:

1. You have a question about some of the information presented during class.

2. You have a question about some of the information in your textbook.

3. You need to turn in a late assignment.

4. You want to get feedback on a paper or assignment you are working on.

5. You don't know how to prepare for an upcoming test.

in the class and how your instructor counts absences and tardies. The withdrawal policy will indicate the last date to withdraw from the class and earn a grade of W. It will also tell you whether the instructor will withdraw students from the class and under what circumstances. Different instructors have different policies about late work; these policies will be clearly identified in the syllabus. For example, some instructors don't accept late work at all while others accept late work but deduct points from the grade for every day that the assignment is late. Finally, the syllabus will also detail how grades in the class are calculated and what grades you can possibly earn. Most syllabi include a list of the major graded assignments and the point values or percentages that the assignments will count toward the final course grade. (See Grades starting on page 187 for more information.)

Each class syllabus also includes an **outline of instruction**, or schedule of class meetings, with varying levels of detail. At the very least, most instructors include a schedule of what content or textbook chapters will be covered in each class meeting. Many instructors also identify when tests and assignments are due. And some instructors also list the homework that is due for each class meeting. This outline of instruction is incredibly useful to students who are taking multiple classes. If you write down all of your test days and assignment due dates in your weekly planner at the beginning of the semester, then you can easily plan for these deadlines and not be surprised when your instructor mentions the test that will take place in the next class meeting.

Keep your syllabus in a safe place like at the very beginning of your class notebook or binder. You should refer to it often as you track your progress in the class. Depending on your instructor's teaching style, she may not remind you of upcoming assignment deadlines or tests. It is your responsibility to come to class prepared to submit work or complete assessments according to the outline of instruction that your instructor provides on the syllabus.

> **Five ways to make every class meeting count:**
>
> 1. Read the textbook and other assigned materials before class, so you will be prepared for the lecture, discussion, and activities. See Chapter 6 for more on reading strategies.
>
> 2. Review your notes from the previous class meetings. See Chapter 7 for tips on making the most of your class notes.
>
> 3. Arrive early and get your notebook, pen, textbook, etc., out before class begins.
>
> 4. Make a list of any questions that you have from the textbook or previous notes, and use the minutes before class begins to ask your instructor these questions.
>
> 5. Go to class even if you are late. It is better to miss half of a class meeting than to miss an entire class meeting.

The Importance of Attendance in College

Your class attendance is a critical part of the learning process in college. Class meetings are your regular opportunities to learn from your instructor and to demonstrate your learning to your instructor. If you must be absent from class, be strategic about when you are absent. For instance, some college students assume that nothing really happens on the first day of class, but this is often an incorrect assumption. On the first day of class, you not only receive the class syllabus and meet your instructor, but you also can get vital information about how the class is organized and what expectations your instructor has of you. Many college instructors also begin teaching the course content on the first day of class, so if you are absent on the first day, then you can find yourself behind in class before you really get started.

Another series of class meetings for which you should prioritize your attendance include the class meeting right before a test or assignment deadline. While few college instructors will dedicate an entire class meeting to preparing for an upcoming test, many instructors will give you guidance on what content to expect to see covered on the test and what kinds of test questions to expect. Instructors may also give you last-minute directions or resources that will help you with an assignment that is due in the next class meeting. Then, of course, you should avoid being absent on the day of the test. Not all college instructors allow for make-up tests, and even if they do, making up a test outside of class can be difficult to schedule. If you must be absent on the day that an assignment is due, then plan to submit your assignment ahead of time or email it to your instructor if possible. Finally, plan to be in class right after the test or assignment deadline or when the instructor returns the graded test or assignment. Your instructor may review the commonly missed test questions, which is a great opportunity to learn from your mistakes and to start to prepare for any upcoming mid-term or final exams. Learning in college is cumulative, which means that concepts build in complexity and difficulty in a single class or course of study, so if you don't understand the concepts on the first test in a class, then you might struggle to understand all future class concepts. If you are absent on the day that your instructor returns the graded tests or assignments, then you miss a chance to learn from your mistakes.

Also, keep in mind that some college instructors give students a grade for their attendance (check your class syllabus to find out if this is true for your instructors). Typically, developmental education and other introductory or pre-requisite classes are most likely to include students' attendance into the overall grade calculation. Even if your instructors do not give you a grade for your attendance, it is possible to fail a class due to poor attendance.

STUDENT NOTES

If you plan to transfer to a university, consider the message your transcript sends when you have a lot of W grades. Your advisor or instructor can help you weigh these factors to determine whether the W is the best option for you.

Student-Initiated Withdrawals

Most community colleges allow students to withdraw from classes until some designated point in the term. If you must miss several class meetings in one semester, consult with your instructor to find out how the absences will affect your grade. Depending on the quantity and timing of the absences, it might be in your best interest to withdraw from the class and receive a grade of W for the class. Just keep in mind that at most community colleges, W grades do impact your financial aid status but do not impact your GPA. Also, note that many community colleges restrict the number of times a student can register for the same course. Specifically, at some colleges you cannot register for the same course more than three times without special permission from the Dean.

Before you withdraw from any class, be sure to talk to your instructor and a financial aid counselor (if you are receiving financial aid). Also, note the last day to withdraw from your classes on your class syllabi. If you choose to withdraw from a class, then you must do so by a certain date depending on the length of the class.

Look for the most up-to-date information about your college's withdrawal policies on the college website.

Faculty-Initiated Withdrawals

Be advised that your instructors may be able to withdraw you from class, too, based on your attendance. At some colleges, instructors must withdraw students from their classes when the students miss a significant portion of the course instruction. Your instructors will tell you on the first day of class and will include in their syllabi exactly how many absences total a significant portion of course instruction. If you have missed several class meetings in a row, then your ability to make up the course content and pass the class is already jeopardized. Again, check the college website for the full policy and the most up-to-date information.

Excused Absences

According to most North Carolina community colleges' attendance and withdrawal policies, "An excused absence is defined as a planned absence." This is a significant change from high school attendance policies. Your college instructors are mostly very sympathetic people who are concerned about your well-being in addition to your education. However, under the current college policy, they are not able to excuse an absence after the fact. You must submit an Excused Absence Notification form at least 14 calendar days in advance to get your absence from class excused. See your college's website for more details about the excused absence policy and for the necessary paperwork.

Grades

Most colleges use the familiar grades of A, B, C, D, and F. At some North Carolina community colleges, students can also earn grades of AU (audit), CE (credit by exam), I (incomplete), P (pass), R (repeat), and NS (no show). Your college's website always has the most up-to-date information about what grades you can earn at the college, and the class syllabus will identify what grades you can earn in a specific class. Many college instructors calculate grades in one of two ways: points or percentages.

Grade Calculations by Points

If your instructor uses **points** to determine your grade in the class, then each assignment will count a certain number of points toward a total number of available points. The table below shows an example of a class with 1,000 available points including points from three tests, a research paper, and a final exam.

Assignment	Points Possible
Test 1	200
Test 2	200
Test 3	200
Research Paper	300
Final Exam	100
TOTAL	1000

If your instructor calculates your grade using points, then you can simply add the points you earn on the individual graded assignments to determine your grade in the class. Then see your class syllabus to find out what letter grade your total point number is equal to. See the following expanded table for an example.

The number of points or the percentage of the total grade assigned to each individual assignment tells you not only how important it is to your overall grade in the course but also how important it is to the learning process in the class.

In the example to the left, the research paper is worth more points than the individual tests or even the final exam. This tells you that your grade on your research paper will have a big impact on your overall grade in the class and that the research paper will be a significant part of your learning process in the class.

Assignment	Points Possible	Your Points Earned
Test 1	200	150
Test 2	200	165
Test 3	200	172
Research Paper	300	225
Final Exam	100	88
TOTAL	**1000**	**800**

The 800 total points earned convert into a letter grade of B according to the table below. For this easy example, you could also divide 800 into 1,000 to convert your points into a grade of 0.80 or 80%.

Points Earned	Letter Grade
900–1000	A
800–899	B
700–799	C
600–699	D
599 or less	F

If you want to calculate your class grade before the end of the semester, you can divide the total number of points you've earned so far by the total number of points possible so far. For example, if you want to know your grade after the first three tests (but before the research paper and final exam), you can add 150, 165, and 172 to get a total of 487 points. Then divide 487 by the 600 points possible so far, and you'll get 0.8116 or 81.16%, which is a grade of B in classes that use a 10-point scale. See the table below for a visual representation of this example.

Assignment	Points Possible	Your Points Earned
Test 1	200	150
Test 2	200	165
Test 3	200	172
TOTAL	**600**	**487**

Grade Calculations by Percentages

Many college instructors use weighted percentages instead of points to calculate students' grades. If your instructor uses **percentages** to determine your grade in the class, then each assignment will count a certain percentage of your total grade. See the next table for an example of a class that has specific percentages assigned to tests, a research paper, and a final exam.

Assignment	Percentage of Total Grade
Tests	50%
Research Paper	30%
Final Exam	20%
TOTAL	**100%**

If your instructor calculates your grade using percentages, then you must multiply your individual grades by the percentages that they count toward the total. Then add these numbers to find your total grade in the class. Look at the expanded table below to see an example. Notice that the table includes three test grades that you must first average to get the overall "tests" grade.

Assignment	Percentage of Total Grade	Your Grades Earned	Percent × Grade
Tests	50%	78, 83, 90 (average = 84)	42
Research Paper	30%	91	27.3
Final Exam	20%	93	18.6
		TOTAL	**87.9%**

To calculate your grade in a class that uses grade percentages, multiply your assignment grades by the percentage of the total.

In the example to the left, multiply 50% (or 0.50) by 84 (average of the three Test grades) to get 42. Repeat the multiplication process for the Research Paper grade (0.30 × 91) and the Final Exam grade (0.20 × 93). Then add 42 + 27.3 + 18.6 to calculate your class grade.

Again, your class syllabus will tell you how to convert the percent grade into a letter grade. Most instructors will round the grade of 87.9% to 88%, which is a B according to the table of 10-point scale common letter grades below.

Percentages	Letter Grade
90%–100%	A
80%–89%	B
70%–79%	C
60%–69%	D
59% or less	F

If you want to calculate your class grade before the end of the semester, follow the steps described above but then divide your grade percentage by the total percentage possible. For example, if you want to know your grade after the first three tests and the research paper (but before the final exam), follow the steps above to multiply your individual grades by the percentages assigned to get 69.3%. This is not your grade.

Assignment	Percentage of Total Grade	Your Grades Earned	Percent × Grade
Tests	50%	78, 83, 90 (average = 84)	42
Research Paper	30%	91	27.3
TOTAL	**80%**		**69.3**

Since Tests (50%) and Research Paper (30%) are 80% of your grade, you must then divide 69.3 by 0.80 because this grade includes only 80% of the total grade for the class. When you divide 69.3 by 0.80, you find that your class grade before the final exam is 87%.

If these examples of two methods of grade calculation are difficult to understand, keep in mind that many instructors will help you figure out how to calculate your grade in their class. If you have a question about how grades are figured in a specific class, then you can always visit your instructor during office hours for clarification. Or you might check the class learning management system website (for example, Blackboard, Moodle, or Sakai) for more information; many instructors post individual assignment grades and running averages on their class websites.

Your Grade Point Average

A **Grade Point Average (GPA)** is a common indicator of success in college. A high GPA will give you eligibility for certain scholarships and honor societies. It will look good on your résumé and will indicate to future employers your strong work ethic. It may also determine whether or not you can transfer to a university or into a specific major.

Most colleges calculate two GPAs that serve two different purposes for its students. At the end of each semester, the college will most likely calculate your cumulative GPA for you, so you can see how your grades in your most recent classes impact your overall GPA. When you graduate, the college will most likely calculate your program GPA as well. Both your cumulative and program GPAs will appear on your official college transcripts which future employers and admissions counselors from other colleges and universities will see.

Your **transcript** is an official record of the classes you enroll in and the grades you earned in those classes at a specific college or university. Most colleges and universities report every class that a student attempts (even if it is for the second or third time) on the transcript. Your transcript sends a powerful message to future institutions of higher learning and to future employers about exactly what kind of college student you were. Therefore, it is important to earn as high a grade as possible in every class you register for, regardless of whether the class is a pre-requisite for your program or a class that is listed on your Plan of Study.

Cumulative GPA

The **cumulative GPA** frequently includes everything the student has ever taken at the college. At some community colleges, the cumulative GPA includes developmental education, other pre-requisite courses, and courses outside of your program of study. However, at other colleges, developmental education courses are not included in GPA calculations. Check with your instructors, advisors, or college website to find out how developmental education classes are considered in GPA calculations.

Consider the following example from a community college where developmental education classes are calculated into students' GPAs. A student takes several courses in the Architectural Technology Associate in Applied Science (AAS) program and then changes her program of study to University Transfer Associate in Arts (AA). She will receive a cumulative GPA that includes her Architectural Technology courses as well as her AA program courses. If she also takes some developmental education courses, then her cumulative GPA will also include her grades in those courses. Your grades in developmental education courses, therefore, are just as important to your cumulative GPA as your grades in the classes that are listed on your Plan of Study.

The cumulative GPA also usually includes every attempt at a class. For example, let's say a student takes MAT 171 twice; he earns a D in the class the first time and a C the second time. Both the D and the C are calculated into his cumulative GPA. Likewise, both grades will likely appear on the student's college transcript.

Program GPA

Unlike the cumulative GPA, the **program GPA** includes only the courses in a student's program of study. So the student who transfers out of Architectural Technology Associate in Applied Science and into Associate in Arts will get a program GPA that excludes her developmental education and Architectural Technology classes. Her program GPA will only include the classes on the AA Plan of Study.

If a student has taken a class more than once, then the program GPA typically includes only the highest grade earned in the class. From the example above, the C in MAT 171 will be calculated into the student's program GPA; his D in MAT 171 will not be calculated into his program GPA.

Although many college students think that you can replace a bad grade with a good grade in your GPA and on your transcript, this is a myth at most colleges. You must take every class seriously and earn the highest grades possible because all of your grades may count toward your cumulative GPA. Likewise, all of your grades appear on your transcript. If you suspect that you cannot pass a particular course, consider withdrawing from it and receiving a grade of W, which isn't calculated into your GPA. Be strategic about withdrawing from classes, though. If you receive financial aid, then you must demonstrate satisfactory academic progress through your program of study. In general, grades of W do not indicate satisfactory academic progress and may negatively impact your financial aid status. See pages 212–214 for more information about financial aid.

Calculating Your GPA

Many community college students can also earn grades of AU, NS, P, R, W, and NS, which do not have any quality points associated with them. Students in developmental education courses may earn the P and R grades. Students who officially withdraw from class within the approved time period earn the W grade.

Always check your class syllabus to see what grades are possible in each of your classes.

Even though the college will probably calculate your GPAs for you, it is important to be able to calculate your own GPA, so you can track your progress during the semester and so you can anticipate the impact a single grade will have on your GPA. It is also beneficial to track your program GPA yourself since it may not be officially calculated by the college until you apply for graduation.

To calculate your GPA, you must know the number of credit hours assigned to each class you take, and you must convert the letter grade you earn into **quality points**. Use the table below to translate letter grades to quality points.

Letter Grade	Quality Points
A	4
B	3
C	2
D	1
F	0

Then multiply the credit hours by the quality points to find the total **grade points**.

Credit Hours × Quality Points = Grade Points

For example, if you make an A in HIS 111 (World Civilizations I, three credit hours), then you can expect to receive 12 grade points for the class because the A is worth four quality points, and three (credit hours) times four (quality points) is 12 (grade points). Add the total grade points for all of the classes you take in a semester and divide the total grade points by the total credit hours in the semester to calculate your GPA.

Total Grade Points ÷ Total Credit Hours = GPA

See the following table for an example. Notice that there are six grade points for ENG 111 because the three credit hours multiplied by the two quality points for the grade of C total six grade points. Similarly, there are nine grade points for PSY 150 because the three credit hours are multiplied by the three quality points for the grade of B. In each row, the credit hours are multiplied by the quality points to determine the total grade points for an individual course. In other words, multiply across but add down to calculate the totals.

Then the total grade points (39) are divided by the total credit hours (12) to calculate a GPA of 3.25.

Course	Credit Hours	Grade	Quality Points	Grade Points
ENG 111	3	C	2	6
PSY 150	3	B	3	9
ACA 122	1	A	4	4
PED 121	1	A	4	4
BIO 111	4	A	4	16
TOTAL	12		TOTAL	39
Total Grade Points ÷ Total Credit Hours = GPA				
39 ÷ 12 = 3.25				

Knowing how to calculate your GPA can also help you understand the impact a single grade in a single class can have on your cumulative GPA. In the following revised example, the student earns a C in ACA 122 instead of an A. This lower grade brings the student's GPA down, but because ACA 122 is only one credit hour, the overall impact is small. Instead of an overall GPA of 3.25, the student's GPA is 3.08.

Course	Credit Hours	Grade	Quality Points	Grade Points
ENG 111	3	C	2	6
PSY 150	3	B	3	9
ACA 122	1	C	2	2
PED 121	1	A	4	4
BIO 111	4	A	4	16
TOTAL	**12**		**TOTAL**	**37**
Total Grade Points ÷ Total Credit Hours = GPA				
37 ÷ 12 = 3.08				

However, a C instead of an A in BIO 111 has a much more substantial impact on the student's GPA because BIO 111 is a four-credit hour class. Compare the following table with the previous table. Earning a C in ACA 122 instead of an A changes the GPA from 3.25 to 3.08. But earning a C in BIO 111 instead of an A changes the GPA from a 3.25 to a 2.58, which is a significant difference. A GPA less than a 3.0 often indicates that a student is struggling in college.

Course	Credit Hours	Grade	Quality Points	Grade Points
ENG 111	3	C	2	6
PSY 150	3	B	3	9
ACA 122	1	A	4	4
PED 121	1	A	4	4
BIO 111	4	C	2	8
TOTAL	**12**		**TOTAL**	**31**
Total Grade Points ÷ Total Credit Hours = GPA				
31 ÷ 12 = 2.58				

You can apply your understanding of how individual grades impact your GPA in two ways. First, when you have to make difficult decisions about which class to prioritize, you should almost always choose the class that has more credit hours associated with it. Inevitably, college students have multiple tests and/or assignments due in the same week. If you haven't managed your time appropriately, then you may have to choose to study for one test more than another test or to complete only one assignment on time. As you make this difficult decision, consider which class will have the bigger impact on your GPA.

Secondly, when you register for classes each semester, consider the impact of three four-credit hour classes if you are trying to build a full-time 12-credit schedule. There are certain advantages to balancing the four-credit hour classes with one- or two-credit hour classes; specifically, you can have a schedule of classes that vary in their demands and so you can better prioritize the higher credit hours. Of course, there are advantages to taking fewer classes, too. Select your schedule strategically to benefit from these advantages.

● Academic Honesty

Institutions of higher education value academic honesty. When many college students consider academic honesty, they think specifically of plagiarism, which is only one important part of academic honesty. **Plagiarism** is the presentation of someone else's words and/or ideas as your own. It is possible to plagiarize purposefully or accidentally, and both are infractions of your college's Academic Honesty Policy. Therefore, college students must educate themselves about their college's Academic Honesty Policy and strategies to avoid plagiarism.

In research papers and class discussions, college students are expected to synthesize what they learn from published articles and books and then make some new points based on the previously published ideas. On assessments and tests, college students are expected to demonstrate their understanding of course content. When students plagiarize or cheat, they violate the college's Academic Honesty Policy, and (just as important) they fail to demonstrate their own learning or understanding of the course material.

STUDENT NOTES

Five Strategies for Avoiding Plagiarism:

1. When conducting research, make photocopies or print-outs of information you want to include in your paper.

2. Use quotation marks around phrases or sentences that you copy word for word from someone else's work.

3. Follow the citation guidelines as required by your instructor (for example, MLA or APA).

4. Don't forget to cite para-phrased material in addition to quoted material.

5. Ask an expert for help. Your instructor, a tutor, or a librarian can help you figure out what you should cite and then how to do so.

Record your goals for your cu-mulative GPA and program GPA on the tracking sheet on page 179 for easy reference in the future.

Students frequently encounter the temptation to plagiarize when they pro-crastinate on assignments or feel overwhelmed by the expectations of a class or of a specific paper assignment. Technology makes plagiarism very easy for students; at the same time, technology makes it easy for instructors to detect plagiarism. It is as easy for your instructors as it is for you to find a paper online or published web articles or opinions.

While some students plagiarize material on purpose, others do so uninten-tionally because they do not know how to appropriately incorporate other people's ideas and writings into their own papers. Be careful to avoid plagia-rism when you quote, paraphrase, and summarize someone else's ideas and/ or words. The best way to avoid plagiarism is by using in-text documentation and a Works Cited or Bibliography page at the end of your paper. Your col-lege English classes will give you many opportunities to practice these writ-ing strategies. Even though you will learn and practice these skills in English classes, your other college instructors will expect you to avoid plagiarism in their classes, too. No matter what program or class you are in, college students are expected to maintain some common standards of academic honesty, including not plagiarizing in writing assignments.

Most Academic Honesty Policies include examples of actions that violate the college's standards in addition to plagiarism. For example, potential violations of a college's Academic Honesty Policy include copying a class-mate's homework, using papers from online paper mills, and working with another person on a take-home test. For the college's Violation Procedure and most current information on the Academic Honesty Policy, see the col-lege website. You may also find your individual instructor's application of the Academic Honesty Policy for his or her class on the class syllabus.

Conclusion

This chapter opened with a brief discussion of how high school and col-lege differ. The common thread among those differences is that in the high school setting, students can rely on teachers—and often parents, guardians, and older siblings—to help them meet their academic expectations. While in college, students are responsible for their own learning and their progres-sion through individual courses and a program of study. When students can effectively read a class syllabus, attend and participate in class regularly, and meet other expectations of adult learners, then they are more likely to be successful in college. Similarly, college students should monitor their aca-demic progressions by anticipating and calculating grades and GPAs. Finally, college provides students with greater expectations for academic honesty and greater consequences when they violate academic honesty policies. As you reflect on how you might apply the information and strategies in this chapter, think specifically about how these concepts will make you a better prepared student and an advocate for your own learning.

CHAPTER 10

College Student Roles and Responsibilities

1. Kourtnie and Kayla are sisters who are taking the same classes this semester: DRE 098, CHM 130/130A, and ACA 122. If Kourtnie earns a B in DRE, an A in CHM, and an A in ACA 122, then what will her GPA be?

> To calculate the GPAs in questions 1 and 2, you need to know that the classes have the following credit hours associated with them:
>
> DRE 098 = 3 SHC
>
> CHM 130/130A = 4 SHC
>
> ACA 122 = 1 SHC
>
> SHC stands for Semester Hours Credit, which is how credit hours are listed on many college documents.

2. Kourtnie and Kayla are sisters who are taking the same classes this semester: DRE 098, CHM 130/130A, and ACA 122. If Kayla earns an R in DRE, a W in CHM, and a B in ACA 122, then what will her GPA be?

3. It is the third week of the semester. Dolly has registered for five courses because she is in a hurry to finish the Fire Protection Technology AAS program. Dolly is in ACA 122, POL 120, ENG 111, developmental math, and CIS 110. She has realized that she cannot be successful in all of the classes at the same time because she also works 30 hours per week and has two small children. She wants to withdraw from one or more of her classes, but she doesn't know which ones to drop. What college policies and procedures does Dolly need to understand to help her make this decision? What advice would you give her?

4. Ramon is taking the same developmental English and reading course for the third time. The first time, he earned an R because he did not complete all of the assignments. The second time, he stopped attending class midway through the semester because he didn't like the instructor. Now he feels pressure to pass the class, so he can begin the college-level requirements for his program. However, he did very poorly on the first test, and he's thinking of withdrawing from the class. What college policies and procedures does Ramon need to understand to help him make this decision? What advice would you give him?

5. Samantha is in ENG 112 this semester. She has always done well in English classes, and so far has an A in ENG 112. However, her first research paper is due in two days, and she hasn't started it yet. While she was researching her topic, she found a paper on the Internet that a student at another college had written. It almost meets the requirements of her assignment, and with only a few small changes, she could turn it in as her own. Samantha wouldn't ordinarily do this kind of thing, but she's in a hurry, and she thinks if she makes enough changes to the paper, then she won't get caught. What college policies and procedures does Samantha need to understand to help her make this decision? What advice would you give her?

6. Read the circled part of the original text below from the Occupational Outlook Handbook. Then read the following sentences and decide which sentences are plagiarized. Assume that the student who wrote the sentences had never heard of respiratory therapy before reading this webpage.

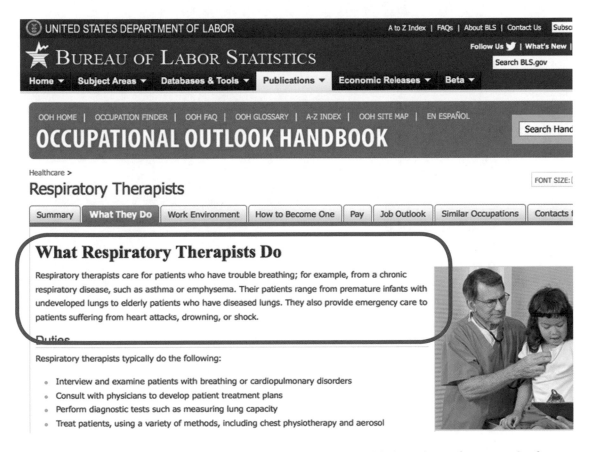

a. Respiratory therapists care for patients who have trouble breathing; for example, from a chronic respiratory disease, such as asthma or emphysema.

b. According to the Occupational Outlook Handbook (http://www.bls.gov/ooh/Healthcare/Respiratory-therapists.htm#tab-2, accessed February 20, 2014), respiratory therapists care for patients who have trouble breathing; for example, from a chronic respiratory disease, such as asthma or emphysema.

c. According to the Occupational Outlook Handbook (http://www.bls.gov/ooh/Healthcare/Respiratory-therapists.htm#tab-2, accessed February 20, 2014), "respiratory therapists care for patients who have trouble breathing; for example, from a chronic respiratory disease, such as asthma or emphysema."

d. Respiratory therapists provide direct care for patients with breathing disorders.

e. Respiratory therapists provide direct care for patients with breathing disorders (http://www.bls.gov/ooh/Healthcare/Respiratory-therapists.htm#tab-2, accessed February 20, 2014).

The College Community

I n addition to learning college policies and procedures, successful college students also know how to navigate and effectively use their campus resources. This chapter will introduce you to some of the most useful campus resources for new college students and will also provide you with helpful tips on how to best use resources available to you. Keep in mind that these resources are available on most community college campuses, but you can always check your campus website, talk to your instructors or advisor, or contact the appropriate department to learn more about your school's specific options. The Contact List at the end of the chapter can help you keep track of your college's specific resources and their points of contact.

Curriculum and Non-Curriculum Courses

Curriculum courses award college credit toward a certificate, diploma, or degree. All courses on your Plan of Study are curriculum courses. The programs that are described in Chapter 2 are all curriculum programs.

Community colleges also offer **non-curriculum courses**, which are classes for personal growth or skills-building and are usually offered through three departments. **Continuing Education** courses are offered by the college to promote lifelong learners who engage in learning to better themselves not only for their careers but also for personal enrichment. Individuals choose to take these classes for self-interest (such as sewing, upholstery, yoga, or sign language classes), licensing or certification (such as vehicle emission inspection, CNA, or personal trainer certification), job training (such as Career Readiness Certificate or Job Skills programs), or to improve basic skills to become more marketable (such as computer or interviewing skills classes).

Non-curriculum classes can also include **Basic Skills** and **English as a Second Language (ESL)** classes, through which individuals may obtain a high school diploma, GED, or English-language skills before enrolling in curriculum courses. No credit is awarded through Continuing Education, Basic Skills, or ESL classes, although individuals in those programs may work toward a completion goal, such as certification or a GED diploma.

While these classes will not directly advance you toward your selected curriculum credential by awarding you curriculum credit, some Continuing Education classes may be of interest to you now. For example, if you are unfamiliar with computers or do not feel confident in your abilities to use word processing software, you may elect to take a keyboarding class or Microsoft Office Word course to prepare you for curriculum courses.

The following information pertains only to curriculum courses, and many of the services described are available only to students enrolled in curriculum courses.

⬤ Class Schedules

North Carolina community colleges offer classes at a variety of times and in a variety of different formats. Many college classes meet two days a week (for example, Mondays and Wednesdays or Tuesdays and Thursdays) for at least one hour each day. You may also find classes meet three days a week (for example, Mondays, Wednesdays, and Fridays) for a little shorter time each day. Rarer are the classes that meet only one day a week. The length of class meetings is determined by the number of contact hours associated with a class and the number of days per week that it meets. Many general education classes are scheduled for mornings, afternoons, and evenings. Some **weekend classes** are even scheduled for Saturdays.

Depending on the academic program, some program classes are offered only during the day or only in the evening. As you explore the many programs available to you at your college, look for terms like "day program" or "evening program" on the Plan of Study to determine when classes within that program are scheduled. You may find that you can complete a program more quickly if you take day classes. Or you may be able to fit your education around your work schedule if you participate in an evening program. Some programs do not give you an option, though, so you will have to take the courses at the pace and in the sequence in which they are required to be completed.

At most NC community colleges, the fall and spring semesters are 16 weeks long. In order to help students move more quickly through their coursework, some classes are scheduled as **mini session** classes, which meet for half of the regular term (eight weeks in 16-week fall and spring semesters, five weeks in 10-week summer terms). These classes cover the same content as the full semester classes, and they meet more frequently (sometimes four days a week). If a class is part of a sequence and it is offered as a mini session, you may be able to complete a two-semester sequence in one semester. For example, GER 111 (Elementary German I) and GER 112 (Elementary German II) may be offered in the same semester. If you register for these classes, then you will take GER 111 in the first eight weeks of the semester and GER 112 in the second eight weeks of the semester (provided that you pass GER 111, of course). If you register for a mini session, you should plan to be very busy with homework, textbook reading, class meetings, test preparation, and assignments for eight weeks. Consider how taking a mini session might affect your other classes as well. You may not want to take a mini session during a semester in which you're taking several other challenging classes.

The **summer terms** vary from college to college, but most often they are eight or ten weeks long. This means that summer classes more closely resemble the fast pace of the mini session than a 16-week fall or spring semester class. When you register for summer classes, anticipate more time in the classroom each week and shorter turnaround times between tests and graded assignment deadlines. For example, if you take a psychology class in fall, then you might have tests every four weeks and papers due every three weeks. If you take the same psychology class in the summer, then you might have tests every other week and only a week and a half between paper deadlines. One good strategy for summer enrollment is to take two classes that you expect to be very interesting and/or very easy to you. Another strategy is to take one class that you expect to be challenging, so you can give that one class all of your attention and focus. Whatever approach you take to summer enrollment, expect your summer instructors to use a more fast-paced approach to instruction and sequence of deadlines.

Instructional Delivery Methods

A large number of college courses are offered in the traditional face-to-face format described above. These are the classes that meet for several hours each week on campus.

In an effort to accommodate students' very busy schedules, some colleges also offer **online courses**. Online courses use the college's learning management system (such as Blackboard, Moodle, or Sakai) for all instructional purposes. Online students log in to the learning management system weekly to complete online assignments, take quizzes and tests, participate on discussion boards, and work through online activities. Most online courses are asynchronous, which means that students can do the work for the course at any time during the week. The instructor and students do not have to be

STUDENT NOTES

Five Strategies for Success in Online and Hybrid Classes:

1. Consider whether your skills and learning style are a good match for online learning. Are you a self-motivated, independent learner with sufficient time management and computer skills?

2. Stay in contact with your instructor. If you have a question about an assignment or course content, email or call your instructor with your questions.

3. Don't wait until the last minute to begin your assignments. If you have technological problems or need help from the instructor, it may be too late to get that help.

4. Schedule time to work on your online class at the same day and time each week.

5. Don't get behind. It is even harder to catch up in an online class.

online at the same time. However, most online classes are not self-paced. Students must work through the course content at the same pace with weekly deadlines to organize their learning.

Online classes offer great flexibility for students with irregular work schedules or other time challenges. But many students report that their online classes seem harder than their traditional, face-to-face classes because they don't have regularly scheduled opportunities to meet with the instructor if they have questions and because online classes require excellent time-management skills. Online classes can also require more time than a face-to-face class might require. Instead of attending class three hours per week and doing five to six hours of homework and class prep, the same class in an online format might require a student to spend 9–12 hours per week reading lecture notes, online resources, discussion board posts, not to mention preparing assignments and studying course content.

If you enroll in an online course, pace yourself. Most online instructors make the weekly activities and assignments available on the same day each week. Check in with the online class on this day every week, so you can see how much work there is and gauge how long it will take you to complete it. Also, get comfortable with the class website early. Different instructors expect students to submit work in different ways (for example, via email, assignments, view/complete, or a digital dropbox). Make sure you know how to use all of the features of the class site before your first assignments are due. Finally, maintain your academic integrity. If your instructor stipulates that you not use your textbook or other materials during a test, then don't. Focus on your learning process, and the good grades will come. Consider, too, the additional strategies in the margin of this page to help you plan for success in an online learning environment.

If you are unsure about whether online classes are right for you, consider taking a hybrid course first. A **hybrid course** features a combination of weekly face-to-face class meetings and weekly online activities and assignments. Keep in mind that the online activities and assignments are not homework for the class meetings; rather, they are part of the class instruction. You will have significantly more work to do outside of class in a hybrid course, but you will have greater time flexibility because many hybrid classes meet face-to-face only once a week. A hybrid course will give you a sense of the online demands of an online course but will also provide you with regular opportunities to meet with your instructor and your classmates.

Self-paced courses are another instructional format, although they are very rare. **Self-paced courses** provide an outline of course expectations, learning objectives, and requirements that the student achieves at his own pace throughout the semester. Often an instructor is available to assist the student with questions, but much of the content is learned independently through a textbook, videos, or online component. Some disciplines, such as math, are more well-suited to self-paced instruction than others. One of the biggest benefits of this learning method includes the ability for students to learn at their own pace, slowing down to spend additional time on concepts they struggle with or advancing quickly through information they already know.

A relatively new instructional delivery method in developmental math at North Carolina community colleges is the **emporium model**. The emporium model requires that students actively participate in the learning process through interactive computer software. Instead of an instructor lecturing from the front of the classroom, the emporium model has students working in a computer lab while the instructor (and usually several tutors or teaching assistants) mingle to answer questions or pull students together for short mini-lessons. Like the self-paced courses described above, students can move quickly through the content that they grasp quickly and move more slowly through the content that is more confusing. But unlike self-paced courses, students in emporium courses must attend class at designated days and times.

Many science, math, foreign language, and career/technical education classes include a lab component. **Labs** give students the opportunity to apply the theories and concepts they learn in the classroom. Labs provide much-needed hands-on practice with new skills and concepts. Depending on the class, your lab may be taught by the same instructor, and your classmates may be the same classmates you see in the lecture or classroom component of the course. Other classes have lab components taught by a different instructor, and only some of your classmates may be in your same lab. However your lab is organized, prepare for labs in the same deliberate, thoughtful way you prepare for class (for example, reviewing your notes ahead of time and preparing lists of questions you want to ask your instructor).

In addition to class time and lab time, many students pursing careers in health can expect to spend time in clinical settings. During **clinicals**, students practice their newly learned skills in a variety of real-world settings under the supervision of an instructor or preceptor. Clinicals give students further opportunities for hands-on practice of the concepts and skills they have learned. Students can also see a variety of departments, workplaces, and specializations that they can pursue after graduation. Many clinical experiences require additional preparation, such as a criminal background check, CPR training, and/or documentation of specific immunizations. When students begin their clinical rotations, they can expect to spend a significant number of hours in the real-world setting. Clinicals can seem like part-time employment (unpaid, of course) in terms of the number of hours required each week.

Another common type of off-campus learning environment that community college students may experience is cooperative education, commonly called **co-op**. Most students in career and technical programs participate in some form of co-op experience. Like clinicals, co-op classes provide students with real-world practice of the skills and concepts they have studied in the classroom. Also, like clinicals, co-op classes can require a substantial time commitment from students. Co-op classes are a great opportunity to practice soft skills, such as punctuality and appropriate workplace language. Some students have leveraged their co-op experiences into full-time employment by demonstrating to the company providing the co-op experience that they are well qualified for the position and demonstrate strong work habits. Even if the co-op doesn't lead to employment, the experience can often provide the hands-on experience that many employers seek and that you can list on your résumé.

Like clinicals and co-ops, service-learning classes offer students the opportunity to apply their knowledge in a real-world setting. **Service learning** includes a volunteer or community service experience that directly supports the learning outcomes of the course and meets a demonstrated need in the community. Unlike required service hours in high school, service learning is a structured service experience with the service clearly corresponding to the material learned in class. If your class has a service-learning component, then your instructor will discuss your service options and expectations and likely guide you through a reflective writing or discussion experience to both prepare for the service learning and then reflect on your experiences.

Finally, some colleges also offer **honors classes** for students who want to participate in advanced learning experiences. Courses designated as honors classes each semester often require independent study components (often an honors project) that are designed in collaboration with the instructor and/or an honors program coordinator or committee. The benefits of taking honors classes include collaborating more closely with instructors, conducting research or improving your depth of understanding on a topic of interest to you, challenging yourself to prepare for future advanced courses, and participating in a program that will impress senior institutions when you apply for transfer. Check your college's website to see if honors classes are offered and the requirements for participation.

Whatever schedule, instructional delivery method, or course format you choose, be sure to select your classes because they are right for you and not because they are the only classes available when you register. Also, keep in mind that online classes are very popular and are often the first classes to fill, so if you want to take a class online, you need to register as early as possible. Talk to your advisor about your readiness for these different instructional delivery methods.

Academic and Personal Support

Your community college recognizes that your success requires additional support beyond the classroom. Numerous academic and personal supports are available to help students address barriers to their achievement. As you read through the following information, think about not only what resources would be of help to you now but also note additional assistance you may seek in the future. When a problem arises, students often find it difficult to manage the concern and also research possible resources. Learning these options now will allow you to act more quickly when difficulties do arise.

Advising

Academic advising is an interactive process that connects each admitted student with a college employee who can guide the student's academic decision making. Often, you are assigned an **academic advisor** after you have been admitted to a program. Advisors may be faculty within your program (for example, if you are in the Health Information Technology program, then your advisor is likely to be an instructor of Health Information Technology courses). Sometimes, advisors are faculty and staff from outside your department who have been trained to advise students in your program. Your relationship with your advisor can be one of the most important relationships you have with a member of the college personnel, but the quality of the relationship depends in large part on you.

At most colleges, you may contact your advisor for assistance at any point in the semester, but new students are almost always required to meet with their advisors in preparation for registration. Before registering for classes each semester, students must meet with an advisor to discuss their academic goals and to receive registration approval for the courses they select each semester. As you successfully progress through pre-requisite courses and into your program, your advisor may allow for this "meeting" each semester to take place over the phone or via email. In many programs, advisors have departmental guidelines that they must follow to determine which students to require face-to-face meetings of and which students to allow some flexibility. Even if your advisor doesn't require a face-to-face meeting for registration approval, you can still request an appointment to discuss your academic and career options. Keep in mind that advisors serve dozens of advisees each semester; make an advising appointment early to be able to get a convenient appointment with your advisor.

Prepare for a successful advising experience by reviewing what is expected of you as the advisee and what you can expect of your advisor.

Advisee Expectations	Advisor Expectations
To take the initiative to contact the advisor about questions or in preparation for an upcoming registration period	To be available to meet with advisees, including on multiple days of the week and at multiple times of the day
To maintain accurate records (see list that follows this table)	To be knowledgeable about the specific program and the college in general
To arrive on time for all scheduled appointments with advisors	To meet all scheduled appointments with advisees
To register for only the classes that the advisor approves based on pre-requisites and co-requisites	To provide sound advice about appropriate course sequences and appropriate course loads
To be forthcoming about progress made in classes and concerns about upcoming classes	To consider the advisee's academic performance in making recommendations regarding registration

Advisees should keep a folder with the following important documents and any other correspondences from the college:

- Any notices of acceptance from the college and/or your specific program of study, which may have been sent as either an email message or a hard copy of a letter sent to your home address

- The Plan of Study you were admitted under

- A Major Pathway or Pre-Major or Study Track (if applicable)

- Your placement test scores (if applicable)

- Unofficial transcripts from any other colleges you have attended (if applicable)

- Your copies of any registration forms you complete with your advisor

- Your Academic Course Plan (see page 78)

In addition to this personal advising relationship, students can take advantage of the expertise of personnel in your college's advising or registration center and transfer center. In these offices, you will find valuable documents, including copies of Plans of Study, Major Pathways, Pre-Majors, Study Tracks, and Bilateral Articulation Agreements as well as information about placement testing, careers that your program is preparing you for, and university catalogs.

University transfer and other students interested in learning about their educational options at senior institutions are especially encouraged to use the college's transfer center and any online transfer information on the college's website. Here you will find information on Major Pathways, Pre-Majors and Study Tracks, Bilateral Articulation Agreements, admissions criteria for area universities, upcoming campus visits by college and university admissions officers, and financial aid.

Tutoring

Many colleges offer tutorial services for students who need additional help with particularly difficult classes. Tutoring varies from campus to campus. Some colleges have peer tutoring through which students tutor other students while other colleges employ professional educators with degrees in the subject they're tutoring (some are even instructors). Some colleges charge students a fee for tutoring; others offer free tutoring to enrolled college students. Some colleges maintain one central center with tables at which you can collaborate with an individual tutor. Others also maintain labs for online tutoring of subjects like math. Check with your college's tutoring center to learn more about how to use this valuable resource at your school, including hours of operation and subjects tutored.

Although tutoring centers vary across North Carolina's community colleges, there are some basic similarities in their operations. For example, keep in mind there are specific actions that the tutors can and cannot do to help you. Specifically, tutors can explain concepts to you and can help you understand directions or assignments. Tutors can also help you interpret instructors' suggestions and corrections on your work. Finally, tutors can help you build confidence in your own abilities and can help you develop study skills.

Keep in mind that the tutor's goal is to help you learn, not to get you a better grade on an assignment. You should not expect the tutors to do your work for you. Their job is to help you better understand the course content, so you can do the work for yourself. Therefore, tutors most likely will not correct or provide answers on assignments that will be graded. Also, tutors cannot predict your grade or tell you what an instructor expects. Finally, tutors cannot complete your assignments for you or help you with take-home exams.

To make the tutoring experience a successful one, bring your textbook, class notes, assignment sheets, and any other class materials that will be helpful. Also, prepare a list of specific questions that you have about the class content or assignment to share with the tutor.

Five Signs You May Need a Tutor:

1. You don't understand how to do your homework.

2. You don't know how to begin an assignment.

3. You earned a low grade on a test or quiz.

4. You suffer from test anxiety.

5. You are easily distracted in class and when you study.

Library

The college library is another useful campus resource, particularly for new college students. If your school has multiple campuses, a library may be available at more than one location. Check your college's website for locations and hours of operation each semester.

Most often, your student ID card serves as your library card, which will allow you to check out circulation materials, use materials on reserve, and access library computers. Circulation materials (including books, CDs, and audiotapes) can usually be checked out for two to four weeks, depending on your library's policies. Renewals are often available and often can be made online, in person, or by phone. Reserve materials (including some textbooks, sample tests and assignments, DVDs, and videotapes) may be used in the library or checked out for a designated time period depending on the instructor's preferences.

In addition to circulation and reserve materials, your library will also have numerous periodicals that will only be available in the library. If you plan to read any of the dozens of current newspapers, magazines, or journals in your library, look for the periodicals section and expect to either read the item in the library or make photocopies of the material.

Your library is also a resource for copying and printing. Photocopying and printing costs vary from campus to campus, so make sure you check posted signs or check with a librarian before you print or make copies. Your library will also likely have a computer lab or access to computers to conduct research and possibly word processing and other software to complete assignments. Your library may also have wireless Internet so that you can bring a laptop to work at one of the study desks located throughout your library.

Interlibrary loan services may be requested to access materials at another library. If you need a specific book or a journal article not available in your campus's library, then your librarian can request the book or article from other community college libraries or from university libraries. Any fees charged to your library for interlibrary loan materials may be passed on to you.

Your library also features access to thousands of research resources through online databases, including NCLIVE, Business Source Premier, ProQuest Science Journals, PsycARTICLES, and Literature Resource Center. These online databases can be accessed from computers on and off campus. Off-campus access is restricted by password, but you can ask a librarian for the passwords you need. Computers on campus allow you to access the online databases without a password. Countless e-books are also available online through NCLIVE. Like the online databases described above, you need a password to access the e-books from off campus.

Your library will also provide helpful information on citation guides, such as MLA, APA, and ASA. This information may be available on your college's library website as well. Your college librarians are familiar with multiple citation guides and can help you avoid plagiarism by citing your sources accurately. See page 195 for more information about avoiding plagiarism.

Remember, librarians are always willing to help students. If you need any assistance, don't hesitate to ask.

Computer Labs

Your college instructors will require that most of your assignments, including all papers, be typed. If you are not already familiar with a word processing program like Microsoft Word, then you may struggle to meet the formatting guidelines for some of your college assignments. Take advantage of online tutorials, the help function in Word, and short courses through Continuing Education programs to improve your word processing skills. Your campus's tutoring center may also offer a computer-use tutor who can help you improve your basic computer skills.

Campus computer labs are intended for educational purposes and offer services to support students' academic goals. In addition to printing abilities, campus labs will also offer Internet access and word-processing software. Additionally, commonly used programs, such as Microsoft Excel or PowerPoint, will be available in most labs. If you don't have a working computer or printer or reliable Internet access, then the computer labs will be a great resource for you. Learn the lab's hours and keep in mind that lab monitors are on duty in several labs to assist with basic computer questions.

Some labs may be designated for use by students in certain programs or classes and will provide hardware and software that are typically utilized in that field or in the course of duties associated with certain jobs. These labs may only be opened to students in specific courses and will likely have shorter hours, so make sure you are aware of the lab schedule and any criteria for use before you make plans to rely on that particular lab to complete an assignment.

Most campuses' computer labs open the first day of classes each semester and are closed on college holidays. Check the specific schedule on your campus. Don't assume the computer lab is always open.

Five Tips for Using Computer Labs on Campus:

1. Save your work on a flash drive or jump drive.

2. Log out of any online programs such as Blackboard, Moodle, Sakai, or email after use. A student who uses the computer after you may be able to access your personal information if you don't sign out.

3. Ask the lab monitor when the computer lab is typically not busy, and then plan your visits accordingly.

4. Find a computer lab before you need it. The worst time to look for a lab is when you are desperate to print a paper right before class.

5. Print only what you need. If you need only 3 pages of a 20-page article, then print only the pages that you want.

Common Computer Lab Policies and Rules:

- Students must present a student ID card to use computer labs.
- While in the lab, students must abide by the college's appropriate use policy and posted lab rules.
- No food or drinks are allowed in the lab.
- Children are not permitted in the lab.
- Loud talking is prohibited and cell phones must be turned off or on vibrate.

Be mindful of the limits on free printing. Some labs charge for all printing; some limit the number of free pages per day or per semester; and some always provide free printing. The policy can vary from lab to lab on your campus. Know the costs before you print.

Wireless Internet access may also be available on your campus, allowing you to access Internet on your laptop at various locations on campus. Check your college website for locations of wireless hotspots where you can access the Internet remotely.

Disability Services

North Carolina community colleges are dedicated to the success of all students. Students with physical, psychological, or learning disabilities may need additional academic supports, which are available through your campus's Disability Services office. Disability Services staff accommodate students with a variety of disabilities through services like individualized educational planning; support staff, including note-takers and interpreters; assistive technology; alternative testing arrangements; and priority assistance during registration. Plan ahead as much as possible to utilize these services since creating the individual plans and providing any required documentation may take several weeks.

Financial Aid

Even though community college tuition is considerably less expensive than tuition at senior institutions, several semesters of tuition can add up quickly. Therefore, the Financial Aid office is one of the first places new students look for when they begin their academic careers. Financial Aid options usually include grants, scholarships, work study, family federal loans and the North Carolina Community College grant and loan program. However, when most people discuss Financial Aid, they usually are speaking of need-based aid, such as Pell grants.

Eligibility for need-based financial aid is based on three factors:

1. financial need,

2. the number of credit hours you are taking, and

3. (sometimes) your program of study.

To find out if you are eligible for financial aid, you must complete and submit the FAFSA (Free Application for Federal Student Aid) online, which is available at http://www.fafsa.ed.gov. Financial Aid staff can provide some help in completing this application if you need it. You must apply early and yearly for financial aid. The best time to apply for financial aid is right after you or your parent(s) (if you are a dependent) file income tax returns. Keep in mind that the process takes longer than most students anticipate.

Students may receive the following sources of financial aid:

■ **Grants:** Grants do not have to be repaid.

■ **Work Study:** The school you attend provides part-time job opportunities that help pay for college.

■ **Scholarships:** Scholarships do not have to be repaid but often have eligibility stipulations.

■ **Direct Loans:** The federal government issues subsidized (need based, lower interest rate) loans and unsubsidized (non-need based and higher interest rate) loans that must be repaid.

Again, keep in mind that acquiring financial aid is a process that takes time and good planning. See a Financial Aid counselor sooner rather than later.

If you receive a financial aid award, then you'll need to demonstrate satisfactory academic progress in order to maintain your financial aid eligibility. **Satisfactory academic progress (SAP)** is defined by the United States Department of Education as meeting the following standards:

1. Maintaining a cumulative grade point average of 2.0 or higher (see page 191 for more information about cumulative GPAs);

2. Maintaining a cumulative credit hour completion rate of 67 percent or higher; and

3. Not attempting more than 150 percent of the course hours required for graduation.

Your cumulative GPA is easy to track each semester. Many NC community colleges post students' GPAs on their WebAdvisor accounts. Log in to see if you meet the minimum standard of 2.0. If you attend a college that doesn't count your developmental education courses in your cumulative GPA, then your college probably does count your developmental education courses in your cumulative GPA for consideration for satisfactory academic progress.

Five Strategies for Maintaining Satisfactory Academic Progress (SAP):

1. Earn a C or better in all of your classes.

2. Before you withdraw from a class, speak to a Financial Aid Officer about how the W grade will impact your completion rate.

3. Only take courses that are listed on your Plan of Study.

4. Take advantage of campus resources, such as counseling and tutoring.

5. Track your cumulative GPA each semester.

You can also track your cumulative credit hour completion rate by dividing the number of credits you complete with grades of A, B, C, and D by the number of credits you attempt. For example, if you register for the following classes and earn the following grades, then your completion rate is 71.4% because you successfully completed 10 of 14 attempted credits.

Course	Credit Hours	Grade
ENG 111	3	A
PSY 150	3	C
MAT 171	4	B
SPA 111/181	4	W

To meet the third standard of Satisfactory Academic Progress, just keep in mind that you will only receive financial aid for 150% of the credits required for your program. For example, if you are enrolled in a 60-credit AA or AS program and you are receiving financial aid, then you will receive enough financial aid to pay for 90 credits (60 credits × 150%). Or if you are enrolled in a 36-credit diploma program and you are receiving financial aid, then you will receive enough financial aid to pay for 54 credits (36 credits × 150%). This should be enough to cover the cost of the courses listed on your Plan of Study as well as any pre-requisite courses you may have to take.

For answers to frequently asked questions, descriptions of the different financial aid sources available, and the most up-to-date financial aid information, see your college's Financial Aid webpage or on-campus office.

Another great resource for college students who have questions about financial aid is the College Foundation of North Carolina (CFNC) website. CFNC has lots of information about the different sources of financial aid (for example, grants, scholarships, and loans) as well as information about the North Carolina 529 Savings Plan for college and some online financial literacy courses.

Academic, Career, and Personal Counseling

No matter how confident you are now in your ability to navigate the college culture and to prepare for your chosen career, read the following descriptions to learn of the many services available to you, most often through your campus's Student Development office. You may be surprised by the diversity and quality of services available.

Academic counseling usually provides educational planning and support for a student's current or future college goals. Academic counseling may be available through several departments on your campus: Admissions, Counseling, Advising, Registration, Transfer, Placement Testing, Student Development, or your program. No matter where your college houses these resources, you should have available to you someone who can provide guidance about choosing a program of study, selecting your courses, developing study skills, discussing transfer options, and/or addressing learning differences.

Career counseling can help students select a fitting professional path that matches their skills, interests, and values. Career counselors can also work with students to determine the steps to reach post-collegiate goals while still a student. Career counseling will most likely be available through a counseling office, student development office, or a career center. Common career counseling topics include finding career fields to match your personality and interest inventories (such as those described in Unit 1), accessing online career resources, learning of available paths to a career, discussing the variety of jobs within a field, advising about current internships and work opportunities, and discussing opportunities to network within the field.

Personal counseling is often limited to your college's counseling center. Because students' academic performance is often affected by their lives outside of the classroom, counseling staff are available to help students manage the aspects of their lives that might interfere with their academic performance. Counselors meet individually with students to provide encouragement and support, intervene in times of crisis, make referrals to community resources when necessary, facilitate relationship and communication skills, and help students identify and resolve personal issues.

Campus Police and Public Safety

Your college's safety office provides protection for college buildings, grounds, and parking lots. The office's safety officers respond to crime reports, fires, medical emergencies, traffic accidents, and other incidents requiring police or security assistance. The office may also provide other valuable services to students, such as creation and distribution of student identification cards and parking decals, first aid for minor injuries, lost and found, and escorts for students on campus at night.

Know the location of your college safety office and its contact information. Your campus may have special phones throughout its campuses to contact the safety office in case of emergency. It's a good idea to make mental note of their locations now in case a need arises.

Veterans' Services

To help veterans understand the policies and procedures pertaining to their education benefits, your college has staff in charge of coordinating and counseling students who are veterans. Contact this coordinator on your campus to learn more about education benefits, including standards of academic progress for veterans and veterans' work study programs. You may also find much of this information on your college's website or on CFNC.org.

Health Services

Your college may offer student health services on campus, which you may contact for minor first-aid treatment or for referrals to community health providers for more significant illnesses or injuries. Your college may also offer health and/or accident insurance. Check to see what your campus in particular offers its student body.

Community Engagement

Five Reasons to Volunteer:

1. You want to learn more about a field before you commit to a program or job.

2. You are new to the area and you want to feel more connected, meet new people, or learn more about where you live.

3. You feel a responsibility to help others and would like to find a way to make a difference in someone's life.

4. You are highly skilled in a specific area, but you want to develop a more well-rounded skillset to appeal to future employers.

5. You are eager to apply what you're learning in the classroom to real life.

The classroom isn't the only place that students can learn and contribute. Your volunteer or community engagement office offers various community service opportunities through which you can apply your skills and academic knowledge through service experiences at a non-profit or government agency. Volunteer work obviously benefits the community served, but it also provides students with important experiences, such as learning new skills, networking with potential employers, developing leadership abilities, and learning to be a part of a team or community. Civic responsibility, community engagement, and volunteering are becoming standard in academic and co-curricular programs at most senior institutions, and students hoping to transfer can improve their candidacy by illustrating a proven record of service to the community. Long-term volunteer commitments are especially impressive to senior institutions and employers.

Student Activities

Student organizations, campus events, and college-sponsored programs provide opportunities to develop friendships, leadership skills, and even job-related experience. Check with your student development or student activities office to learn more about your college's offerings, and take advantage of those that interest you.

Student Clubs and Organizations

Student groups provide excellent opportunities to get involved on campus, make new friends, network with students in your academic program, and build your leadership skills. Your membership in service organizations and honor societies, in particular, demonstrates your dedication to your academics and future career field. Participation in some of the organizations is by invitation only based on your academic standing or program enrollment.

See your college's website for information on how to get involved in student clubs and organizations. While you are there, look for links to the individual clubs for meeting times and locations. You may also find this information on bulletin boards around campus, especially in the student services building on your campus.

Student Government

Your college will have a student government (often called the Student Government Association or Student Senate) that will coordinate and regulate activities and issues of concern to all students at your college. The organization represents students' voice as the official student government association on campus. Likely, the student leadership group meets monthly to discuss campus concerns, regulate campus activities, review or create procedures involving student organizations and activities, and respond to campus regulations that affect the student body as a whole. If you are interested in developing your leadership skills and participating fully in the college's student life, consider joining your campus's student government group.

Sports

Additionally, your campus may have intercollegiate sports teams that you can join. Many NC community colleges compete against other colleges within the National Junior College Athletic Association's Region X in such sports as basketball, baseball, softball, golf, volleyball, and cross country. Check with your school to learn about upcoming games you can attend or to learn of opportunities to play collegiate sports, including information about trying out for the teams.

Campus Events

Your Student Development or Student Activities office (often in partnership with student clubs, organizations, or student government groups) will sponsor college-wide student events on campus. These events provide great opportunities to learn about the college's clubs and organizations, enjoy food and drinks with your classmates, and build a sense of community on campus. Look for information about these events, especially around the beginning of the academic year.

◼ Conclusion

Revisit the tracking sheet on page 179 to personalize the content in this chapter.

Your college is committed to helping its students succeed. Your college purposefully offers its classes in a variety of schedules and instructional delivery formats, so students can learn effectively and efficiently. To support the learning process, your college also offers a variety of campus resources to support your success, such as tutoring, library services, computer labs, academic advising, financial aid, counseling, campus safety, veterans' services, health services, and student activities, clubs, and organizations. Please check your college's website for additional resources and the most up-to-date information about the resources described in this chapter.

CHAPTER 11
The College Community

REVIEW QUESTIONS

1. Match the person(s) on campus who could help in each situation. More than one response may be correct.

   1) Instructor   **a.** You were absent from class and want to get the class notes.

   2) Advisor   **b.** You need help preparing for an upcoming test.

   3) Tutor   **c.** You are having doubts about your career goals and are considering changing your program.

   4) Counselor

   5) Classmate   **d.** You have a question about one of the concepts in your textbook.

       e. You have gotten over a week behind in all of your classes and are experiencing extreme stress.

2. Imagine the ideal college campus. What offices, services, and other resources does your definition of an ideal college campus have?

3. Locate your college's mission on your college's website or in your student handbook. How do the college's campus resources serve the college's mission? Are there any additional resources that the college should offer in order to better fulfill its mission?

4. Find a list of student clubs and organizations on your campus. What are two that you're interested in joining now or in the future?

5. Samuel has worked as a lab technician in a research facility for over five years and is very self-directed and intelligent. However, he is experiencing some difficulties in his first semester in college. First of all, he is struggling in his math class because it has been so many years since he has studied algebra. Also, he wants to get more involved in campus life, but he hasn't had much success making friends in his classes. Finally, he isn't sure which degree program he should be in because he is considering transferring to a university. What resources in his college community should he explore to address each of his challenges? Why?

My Campus Contact List

Whom Do I Contact for...	Department	Location	Contact Information
Academic Advising			
Academic Records			
Applying for Graduation			
Career Counseling			
Changing Programs			
Disability Services			
English as a Second Language Services			
Financial Aid Counseling			
Instructional Concerns			
Insurance Information			

Whom Do I Contact for...	Department	Location	Contact Information
International Student Services			
Lost and Found			
Parking Permits			
Parking Ticket Payment			
Registration			
Scholarships			
Security			
Student Events/Activities			
Testing			
Textbooks			
Transcripts			

Whom Do I Contact for...	Department	Location	Contact Information
Transfer Information			
Tutoring			
Veterans' Education Benefits			
Withdrawing from a Class			
Work Study Programs			
As you identify additional resources you may need to contact on your campus, add that information below.			

Conclusion:
Putting It All Together

A s you near the end of your college success class, consider how you will synthesize everything you've learned to help you prepare for the end of the semester and the beginning of the next semester. The end of the semester is an excellent time to assess how well this semester went. For example, did you manage your time effectively to meet your goals and deadlines? Did you take an appropriate number of classes? Did you make use of the resources available to you at optimal times of the semester? To help with this assessment, consider the following information as you put all the pieces together.

Registration for Next Semester

Register as early as possible for the coming semester, so you can increase your chances of taking the classes you want in the instructional delivery format you want them (for example, online or mini session classes). Registering early also gives you more choices in class schedules (for example, day, evening, or weekend classes). If you haven't yet met with your advisor this semester, you should make an appointment with him or her as soon as possible. Then register for next semester's classes as soon as you are eligible to.

As you prepare to meet with an advisor and to select a schedule for the next semester, reflect on how well you managed your course load this semester. If you were a full-time student, how well did you balance your schoolwork and your other responsibilities like family and work? Should you take one (or two) fewer classes next semester to avoid burnout? If you were a part-time student, could you take more classes next semester to move more quickly through your Plan of Study? Or have you set a pace that will allow you to complete your credential with relatively little stress?

Remember, too, the impact of each course grade on your cumulative GPA. It may be a good idea to take fewer classes, so you can earn higher grades, and maintain (or improve upon) the GPA you will earn this semester.

When you meet with your advisor, take your completed Academic Course Plan with you (see page 78). Your advisor is an excellent source of information about pre-requisites and co-requisites. Also, your advisor can give you more information about when your program classes are offered (for example, only in the fall semester or only in the summer term).

New Resources

If this is your first semester at your college, then you may have participated in a new student orientation before you registered for classes. Now that you are a returning student, you will not need to participate in another orientation. Instead, you will meet with your assigned advisor, take advantage of your college's advising and registration center, or meet with a campus transfer counselor. You may also consider seeking the advice of your instructors, who can be excellent advising resources if you have a quick question before or after class. For in-depth questions that involve your personal progress through your program or any analysis of your transcript, always go to your assigned advisor first.

Experimenting with New Learning Strategies

Success by Design and your college success course introduced you to dozens of new learning strategies, such as time-management techniques, note-taking strategies, and study skills. Most likely, you have not had the opportunity to try all of these strategies this semester. Consider keeping this textbook even after the class ends and referring back to the strategies that you haven't yet tried out.

You may have had the experience of taking fairly easy classes this semester in which you didn't need to use any learning strategies other than those that were already familiar to you. In future semesters, as you take more and more difficult classes, you may want to be able to remember the individual strategies described in this book. Or your first semester of college may have been so difficult and overwhelming that you found two or three techniques that worked for you and then used them over and over. Remember that successful students have a whole repertoire of learning strategies that they can apply in different classes and for different purposes. Even after this class ends, you should continue to develop your personal repertoire of effective learning strategies.

Reflections on Personal Experiences

Finally, evaluate your experiences by reviewing the following table of characteristics of successful and struggling students. To assess yourself, read the table and highlight or underline the characteristics of successful students that you identify with. Then use a different color to highlight or underline the characteristics of struggling students that you identify with. Hopefully, at this point in the semester, you identify with more of the characteristics of successful students. As you continue to develop as a student, keep in mind the areas you can improve. Remember, too, that even after this class ends, you will have access to many campus resources to continue developing successful attitudes and characteristics.

Successful Students	Struggling Students
☑ Have a clear motivation that guides their goals and provides incentive for their day-to-day work	☒ Don't clearly see the meaning in their actions or current paths ☒ Don't have clear goals and don't know the specific steps to get where they want to go
☑ Know a wide variety of strategies to use and are flexible in selecting the best method for a situation	☒ Have few strategies at their disposal and often feel stuck or discouraged if their methods do not work
☑ Manage their day-to-day tasks while also keeping an eye on the future, prioritizing items by urgency and importance	☒ Respond to the task that elicits the most stress ☒ React rather than plan and manage
☑ Take initiative to complete tasks	☒ Wait to be told to do something
☑ Divide tasks into smaller pieces and establish a plan to accomplish the individual items on time	☒ Feel overwhelmed by the size of the task ☒ Wait until the last minute to start large projects, thereby causing themselves more stress and harming their results
☑ Expect the unexpected to arise	☒ Are derailed by unwanted or unplanned events
☑ Consider new information and other points of view in order to understand	☒ See opposing ideas or different methods as an attack or challenge to their beliefs and preferences ☒ Resist new ideas or methods
☑ Seek support and resources ☑ See assistance as a helpful and valuable tool	☒ Do not seek support ☒ See services as an indication of a personal weakness

(continued)

Successful Students	Struggling Students
☑ Evaluate their learning by thinking about how they learn best ☑ Personalize their learning according to their specific needs, such as selecting their study methods according to their learning style preferences	☒ Do not think about how they learn ☒ Blame the instructor or textbook if they do not do well ☒ Feel their learning is mostly the instructors' responsibility ☒ Assume there's only one way to learn
☑ Expect that they must supplement classroom instruction to learn	☒ Assume that learning occurs only during class
☑ Believe they can accomplish their goals	☒ Make self-defeating assumptions, such as feeling inadequate or unworthy ☒ Repeat negative self-statements, such as "I'm a bad tester" or "I can't learn math"
☑ See setbacks, lack of success, or struggles as a challenge that can be overcome	☒ Assume problems cannot be solved ☒ Attribute problems to a personal flaw
☑ Can leave personal situations, emotional stress, or other difficulties at the classroom door in order to focus on learning	☒ Feel controlled by their emotions ☒ Allow their emotions to interfere with their learning
☑ See learning as a life-long adventure ☑ Have a natural curiosity that creates a desire to learn ☑ Find something interesting in nearly everything they encounter	☒ See learning only as a means to an end ☒ Do not value mental play, critical thinking, or other less immediate—but still important—benefits of education
☑ Find a way to connect personally to material	☒ Fail to see connections between the material and daily life

Index

About the Authors

Gabby McCutchen is Assistant Dean for the Student Engagement and Transitions department and Chair for the First-Year Experience at Durham Technical Community College. She led the curriculum development for ACA 085, ACA 111, and ACA 122 at Durham Tech. She has taught over 100 sections of ACA 111 and ACA 122 since 2006, and has trained over 150 college faculty and staff to teach ACA. Gabby led the writing of the goal exploration and college culture units.

Erin Riney has been teaching ACA at Durham Technical Community College since 2009. In addition to her ACA and Developmental English and Reading teaching duties, Erin serves as Service-Learning Coordinator at the college, directing campus-wide community engagement efforts. Erin has worked for over a decade as a private tutor, including eight years spent tutoring thousands of SAT, ACT, and MCAT students as a Master Tutor for a leading test prep company in Indiana, Kentucky, North Carolina, and the DC-metro area. Erin led the writing of the learning strategies chapters, including the reading, study, and test-taking chapters.